PARENTING

—— for the ——

LAUNCH

RAISING TEENS TO SUCCEED
IN THE REAL WORLD

Dennis Trittin AND Arlyn Lawrence

LifeSmart

PUBLISHING, LLC

Praise For *Parenting for the Launch*

This book is a must read for parents of teens. In a comfortable and engaging style, Trittin and Lawrence offer valuable guidance to parents confronting the transition of their kids to adulthood. The book is inspirational and practical, insightful and encouraging. As parents, it is both our obligation and our great privilege to help our teens prepare for the years ahead, and all parents hope and pray for the knowledge and skills and courage to set their teens on the path to success. This book is a wonderful tool to help equip parents for that responsibility.

Troy Alstead, Group President & Chief Financial Officer, Starbucks Coffee Company

Dennis and Arlyn have once again delivered a book full of invaluable insights and practical strategies for parents who want to help their children succeed. You'll find dozens of great ideas for preparing your son or daughter to hit the ground running when it's time to enter the world of work and tackle an adult life full of challenge and change. It's never too early to start building a strong relationship with your child—in this book you'll find many ways to weave in a sense of purpose and direction to create the best future possible for this amazing kid who's about to change the world!

Cynthia Ulrich Tobias, M. Ed, Author & Speaker

The greatest investment we can make in our teens is to prepare them well and release them with confidence to their own future. Dennis and Arlyn have given us the essential principles and a practical game plan for doing exactly that in this must-have parenting guide. This is the book that parents of teens have been waiting for!

Jeff Kemp, Former NFL Quarterback and Vice President, Family Life

Today's busier, faster society is waging an undeclared war on our teenagers. In their new book, Dennis and Arlyn have provided an anchor for parents on how to prepare, plan, and launch their child into the real world. This is a must-read for any parent raising a teenager!

Noel Meador, Executive Director, Stronger Families

This is an awesome book for parents! It is filled with such great advice for how to "prepare and let go" when our teens don't always want to listen. I especially appreciated the strategies for building stronger relationships through personality profiling and affirming their uniqueness and value. *Parenting for the Launch* and *What I Wish I Knew at 18* is the perfect set for parents to raise well-prepared, self-confident young adults.

Pam Wickman, High School Life Skills Teacher

This is the book for parents who are ready to be coached on how to build character and confidence in their children. Like all great coaches, Dennis Trittin and Arlyn Lawrence balance teaching and training, principles and personal stories, powerful insights and practical ideas. Their game plan builds upon simple truths that result in strategic goals. They recognize that confident, launch-ready children need parents who apply proven leadership principles to their own lives before applying them to their kids. Each chapter is a muscle-building exercise for mothers and fathers who aspire to lead their children into becoming difference-makers.

Phil Miglioratti, COO, Mission America Coalition

As one who has worked with the younger generation for 45 years, I applaud Dennis and Arlyn for their articulate approach to empowering parents to be focused and intentional—especially when navigating those formative years when boys and girls are becoming men and women. We as committed and loving parents need all the help we can get to nurture and challenge our kids in the adolescent years of life. Well done!

Doug Burleigh, Past President, Young Life

It has taken my husband and me years to figure out some of the concepts that fill this book. You will gain insight into how to provide a solid foundation that will inspire your children to learn, have greater confidence, make beneficial decisions, be more "other-focused," and take joy in contributing to the world around them. We would have enjoyed reading it in the early years of parenting our now-adult children! By writing this book, Dennis and Arlyn are richly blessing the parents who read it as well as the children whose parents follow its wise counsel.

Linda Olson, Managing Director, Cornerstone Advisors

When hiring new employees, it can be challenging to find young men and women that have benefitted from proactive parents who prepared them to succeed in today's dynamic business world. As a father of teenagers, I am keenly aware of the challenges my wife and I face with preparing our kids emotionally, intellectually, and spiritually for their journey ahead. Dennis and Arlyn have hit on the essential principles to guide moms and dads to successfully develop and "graduate" their children to college and the workforce.

John Carpenter, Vice President, Weyerhaeuser Corporation

What a powerful book! Personal, engaging, and entertaining, Dennis and Arlyn offer sound guidance for parents, families, mentors, and educators who are equipping young people for adulthood.

Willie Stewart, Retired Public School Administrator

This is a book about successful parenting written by successful parents with integrity who freely share their insights with humility. Dennis and Arlyn provoke our thoughts and question our assumptions as parents. When you finish studying *Parenting for the Launch*, you'll have a whole new arsenal of insights and methods for the next phase of your parenting career.

Richard P. Himmer, Organizational Consultant, Family Coach, Author

Dennis and Arlyn have hit the mark for parents raising teens. This book is filled with compelling ideas for building a leadership foundation and relating to my own teenager. Adjusting my communications to his behavioral style will help cultivate mutual trust and understanding during these critical years. Thank you!

Joseph Helms, Managing Director, Ronald Blue & Co.

In *Parenting for the Launch*, Dennis and Arlyn provide wisdom that is insightful and applicable—but they don't stop there. This book will serve you well as a valuable road map to assist you in the weighty but rewarding charge as parents—to prepare your child for his or her launch into the "real world."

Mike Riches, Pastor, Author, International Speaker

Parenting for the Launch: Raising Teens to Succeed in the Real World
First Edition Trade Book, 2013

Published by LifeSmart Publishing, LLC. Gig Harbor, WA 98332.

To order additional books:
www.parentingforthelaunch.com
www.dennistrittin.com
www.atlasbooks.com
www.amazon.com

Or:

Via email: orders@bookmasters.com

Via phone: 1-800-Booklog (1-800-266-5564), a 24/7 order line

Via fax: 1-419-281-6883

Via mail:
BookMasters, Inc.
P.O. Box 388
Ashland, Ohio 44805

ISBN: 978-0-9832526-7-2
Book Packaging: Scribe Book Company, Nashville, TN
Book Design: Susan Browne, Nashville, TN
Printed in the USA by BookMasters, Inc., Ashland, OH
Atlasbooks, distributor

We dedicate this book to our families:

. . . to our parents, with deep gratitude for investing their lives in us and for being great role models.

. . . to our spouses, with love and appreciation for partnering with us in life and parenting.

. . . to our children, with pride and awe that, despite our imperfections and mistakes, you have grown into such incredible people. Your lives are our credibility. We are so very proud of you.

ACKNOWLEDGMENTS

We are profoundly grateful for the inspiration, encouragement, and support we have received from so many people along our journey.

We would like to acknowledge and honor the LifeSmart team of Susan Browne, Dan DePriest, Corey Foster, Tom Jonez, Doug Lawrence, John Thompson, Jeanne Trittin, and Mike Trittin for their wisdom, encouragement, and service. Your total commitment to excellence and our mission have been tremendous gifts to us.

We would also like to honor the many friends who have been invaluable to us through their advocacy and ambassadorship of our work and mission: Gaylord Anderson, Doug Burleigh, Bill Cantus, Dean Curry, Bill Findley, Toni Fitzpenn, Chris Gilge, Joe Helms, Teri Hickel, Tom Kamp, Jeff Kemp, Ed McCahill, Bea McLeod, Noel Meador, Darrin Miller, Curt Morford, Trisha Novotny, Fred Oldenburg, Linda Olson, Wayne Perryman, Laura Prinsloo, Mike Riches, Ted Robinson, Debbie Schindler, Missy Scudder, Denis Stanislaus, Willie Stewart, Cynthia Tobias, Mark Toone, Pam Wickman, Cindi Witt, Tom Van Riper, and Andy Wyatt.

You have extended the impact of our work further than we could have ever imagined—touching lives and empowering the next generation from our hometown to around the world. We are grateful!

MEET THE AUTHORS

We are Dennis Trittin and Arlyn Lawrence., an author/publisher and writer/ editor who started collaborating when Dennis penned *What I Wish I Knew at 18: Life Lessons for the Road Ahead*. We quickly discovered a common passion for equipping and empowering young adults, and for bringing practical resources and encouragement to those who guide them—parents, educators, and youth mentors.

Subsequently, Dennis founded LifeSmart Publishing and together we developed the *What I Wish I Knew at 18* Leadership and Life Skills curriculum. The book and our course are now inspiring families, schools, and youth mentoring organizations around the country—and around the world!

Both of us were raised in strong families and have strong, grown families of our own. We know the influence and impact that healthy, intentional parenting can have on children. At the same time, through our work with educators, counselors, mentor organizations, and families, we see the huge need for more parents to be equipped and encouraged in this vital role. This is especially true as kids approach the middle to late teen years and their departure for the "real world" looms on the horizon.

Don't be surprised if you feel a little convicted when you read our book . . . we certainly experienced a lot of conviction in writing it! We, along with our spouses, will be the first to tell you we are not perfect parents, nor do we have perfect children. We would all love the opportunity for some "do-overs!" But the goal is not to be perfect parents, just *better* parents. And we can certainly all aspire to that, can't we?

We bring unique perspectives to the parenting conversation. Our past roles—Dennis in business leadership and Arlyn in child and family development—gave us valuable lenses through which to view leadership and life preparedness training. Our current roles put us squarely in the thought arena of what is happening "out there" with young people now. Because we're involved in the educator, business, and mentor communities, we hear their feedback about the training today's kids are *not* getting, and what's needed—from the perspectives of those receiving the kids we are raising (i.e., schools, colleges, youth organizations, and employers). And, as part of a community of parents ourselves, we are also keenly aware of the emotions and concerns that surround the launching and releasing of our children into society—out of our arms and into the real world.

Some of the concepts you will see here are original. Many are derived from among the most innovative parenting and youth development strategies of other thought leaders. We hope you'll find all of them as thought provoking and beneficial as we have.

Being called to this mission is something of a surprise for us, but it is one to which we feel passionately committed. It's our joy and privilege to serve other parents, who, like us, want to set their children up for every success in life.

 **Dennis Trittin** / Prior to his most recent career as an author, publisher, educator, mentor, and speaker, Dennis was a successful investment manager and senior executive for 28 years with Russell Investments. During his career, Dennis researched and evaluated thousands of investment leaders worldwide, giving him a unique perspective to share the strategies and practices of successful people.

Dennis holds a Bachelor of Business Administration (B.B.A.) from the University of Wisconsin and a Master of Business Administration (M.B.A.) in Finance from the University of Washington, where he was Valedictorian of his class. He also holds a Chartered Financial Analyst (C.F.A.) designation.

A frequent speaker at educator and family conferences on the topics of leadership and preparing young people for life success, Dennis is a passionate advocate for providing kids with the best possible launch into adulthood. He is also dedicated to promoting the educational and cultural shifts that may be necessary to achieve that goal on a national level. He has served as a board chair, a finance and life skills teacher at Lighthouse Christian School, and as a deacon at his church. He also serves as a regular advisor to a number of non-profit organizations.

On the home front, Dennis has been married to his wife, Jeanne, for 31 years. They have two grown children and make their home in Gig Harbor, Washington.

 **Arlyn Lawrence** / is the editor, curriculum developer and seminar leader for LifeSmart Publishing, including the *What I Wish I* Knew *at 18* book and leadership course. Her background in publishing includes freelance writing and editing, curriculum development, and a five-year stint as a magazine columnist and editor, as well as her current work as a book editor and publishing project manager. A published author and international seminar leader emphasizing children and family leadership, she equips parents and educators with vision, perspective, and practical solutions. She is a graduate of the University of Maryland.

Arlyn spent fourteen years homeschooling her five children before they entered the public school system, and over fifteen years as an educational director for youth and children's programming. She and her husband, Doug, have been married for 30 years and, in addition to their five children, are delighted to have one granddaughter and another on the way. They reside in Gig Harbor, Washington.

CONTENTS

INTRODUCTION

*Before I got married I had six theories about bringing
up children; now I have six children, and no theories.*
John Wilmot

Few transitions bring as much joy, tears, and anxiety to parents as when
their children graduate from high school and head off into the "real world."
It's a strange concoction of emotions that is one part reflection (all the
memories), one part conviction (did we do everything we could?), and one
part wonder (how will they do?). Questions race through your mind:

"Have I taught them everything they need to know?"

"Are they on the right track?"

"Will they make good decisions?"

"How will our relationship change?"

"Can they live successfully as independent adults?"

"Are they ready?"

"Am I ready???"

As a parent, you play the vital role in preparing your teen for a successful launch. No doubt the past fifteen, sixteen, seventeen years or so
have flown by quickly. Now, you're on the verge of seeing him or her off
into the next season of life. If you're like us—and most of the other parents we meet—you want to make sure you've done everything you can to
set him or her up for success.

It's a tall order indeed, and what compelled us to write this book. The
teen years offer special challenges and opportunities, because our children
are changing so much (seeking and expressing independence and establishing their identities) and there are SO many decisions to be made. The

responsibilities of preparing them for independent living, while building a relationship that will endure forever, can feel overwhelming (especially when other voices seem to have greater influence than ours). And, while there are many excellent parenting books out there, many focus on behavior and discipline without offering the complete picture of life readiness.

These days, the stakes are higher for young adults making their way into the world. For the first time in decades, the next generation will not necessarily live a more secure and affluent lifestyle than its parents. Many would argue that economic and cultural forces have made today's world a more formidable environment than most of us experienced at that age. We agree.

In our work with educators, businesses, mentor and faith organizations, and at-risk youth programs, we have heard a resounding plea for parents and those who guide our youth to work together to equip and empower the next generation. It is an urgent situation. Colleges and employers report that an alarming percentage of today's graduates are ill-equipped to handle the pressures and responsibilities of the real world. This was yet another motivation for writing this book. As our world is becoming more competitive, our younger generation is often lacking the personal skills to succeed. We can, and must, do better.

Kids today need more than head knowledge. They need a solid, holistic leadership foundation that will support them and enable them to make key decisions in these crucial years and beyond. This includes having a purposeful life perspective, solid character, strong personal disciplines, the ability to develop healthy relationships, career smarts, financial management skills, and the capacity to overcome adversity. This book will help build the foundation your teen needs to flourish in all aspects of life.

Teens may pick up some tips at school or elsewhere, but guess what, parents—it starts with you! The good thing is, YOU are the most qualified for the job. No one else knows your teen like you do. And no one else's voice matters as much (whether you feel like it or not).

We wrote this book for you as a road map for a successful launch of your teen into the real world—whether it be to college, the workplace, the military, service, or elsewhere. It can help bring clarity to your parenting goals and offer direction and innovative strategies to achieve them. Whether your relationship with your teen is rock solid or strained, our hope is that our message inspires and equips you for the greatest of successes—and a relationship with your adult child that will only grow stronger and more rewarding as the years go by.

One more note: *Parenting for the Launch* can be used as a stand-alone parenting guide, or, ideally, in conjunction with our companion book, *What I Wish I Knew at 18: Life Lessons for the Road Ahead. Parenting for the Launch* is directed to toward you, the parent, and gives a global framework for how to approach and execute the launch. *What I Wish I Knew at 18*, on the other hand, is messaged directly to your teen. It has the nuts and bolts, if you will, of the success principles you'll want to communicate before your son or daughter leaves home. We recommend you use both books for maximum impact.

Letting go of a young adult child can be hard—and it always seems to come sooner than you think. When it does happen, as it inevitably will, we want to give them wings—not strings! We want to let them go with confidence and watch them soar to success in every area of their lives.

That's our mission, and we're glad you've joined us by picking up this book. Here's to the successful launch of YOUR teen!

Part One:

Destination Preparation

GIVE THEM WINGS, NOT STRINGS

KEEP YOUR EYES ON THE GOAL

BUILD A SOLID LEADERSHIP FOUNDATION

PREPARE THEM FOR KEY LIFE DECISIONS

"Did we cover all the bases?"

It's perhaps the most fundamental (and scary) question parents ask when launching their teen into independence. The subject arenas are so vast, from leadership to relationships to productivity to adversity, not to mention key life decisions such as college, career, family, and finances. The responsibility can feel overwhelming at times.

The next four chapters are designed to help you to confidently cover the bases. You'll learn about:

1. giving your teen wings to soar as you gradually release control
2. identifying your goals as you raise future adults
3. building a solid personal leadership foundation in your teen
4. providing before-the-fact wisdom for the key life decisions they'll soon be making

This is "beginning with the end in mind" (a là Steven Covey), which is a great mindset in which to operate when raising teenagers. In our busy lifestyles, very few stop to ask the defining questions of "Where are we headed?" and "How will we know when we get there?" This section will help you develop answers to these key questions, and establish the guiding principles for a successful launch of your teen into the real world.

CHAPTER ONE

GIVE THEM WINGS, NOT STRINGS

The greatest gifts you can give your children are the roots of responsibility and the wings of independence.
Denis Waitley

When my (Arlyn) minute-old son was placed in my arms after a 12-hour labor, the doctor and nurses told us, "Congratulations!" while my husband Doug danced with elation. After the hubbub finally subsided and everyone else had left my hospital room, I lay in the dimness and gazed at our now-sleeping newborn in the bassinet beside my bed. In an instant, my life had totally changed. We had brought this child into the world and he was totally dependent on us. Pure awe—and total overwhelmed-ness.

Now fast forward twenty-one years.

Tyler had just graduated from college and was ready to start his first job as a land use planner in a city three hours away. We all helped him move—Doug, me, and our four younger children, then aged 18, 16, 13, and 10. We loaded up a U-Haul with his belongings and meager furnishings, drove over the mountains to Eastern Washington, and moved him into his new digs.

The first night, we were packed like sardines into the one-bedroom apartment. Doug and I were sleeping on a futon, with Tyler on the floor directly to my right—the same position in which he had rested beside me 21 years earlier, that first night of his life.

As I watched this now six-foot man sleep, it struck me how quickly these 21 years had flown by. Now here he was, about to start life on his own. My feelings were as weighty then as the day I embarked on my parenting career. In fact, they were even stronger, as we now had a 21-year history of relationship and experiences between us. How would we all handle this new season of life?

That was when I realized: You never *stop* being a parent. And you never *arrive*. You never really *want* to let go. But you eventually *have* to. This is, after all, why we raise them up—to *release* them to fulfill their dreams and purpose.

Our goal as parents when that day comes? They soar!

HOW DID WE GET HERE SO QUICKLY?

With each of my kids, I have been surprised by how quickly the launch date arrived. They don't stay babies for very long and before you know it they're teenagers. Zero to 18 in no time flat! Then off they go.

Remember how, when you or your partner were first expecting, you likely read books, talked to other new parents, and maybe quizzed your own parents? You fixed up the nursery just in time for the Arrival. "Expecting" a young adult is no less momentous—there just isn't a specific arrival date. In fact, if you're not careful, it sneaks up on you. One day they're playing dress-up and Legos®, watching cartoons, playing ball with you in the back yard, and wanting you to tuck them into bed at night. The next thing you know (or so it seems), they're into makeup, designer jeans and shoes, cell phones, video games, and dating! Their friends displace you as the VIPs in their lives. You can go days—weeks—without a meaningful conversation. This can blindside you, if you're not prepared.

The years leading up to the launch constitute a season of parenting some might call the "best of times and the worst of times," as Charles Dickens put it. It helps to be well prepared. It's good to know your goals and objectives in advance—and how you're going to accomplish them. You need to objectively know your teen—and yourself. You'll want to have a strong relationship with him or her and be able to communicate effectively. Admittedly, none of this is for the faint of heart, and nothing we probably ever thought about when we considered having a family.

However, you don't have to fear the teen years. Don't let other people's negative experiences or worst-case scenarios scare you. No one else's story is your story. And, no one else's teen is *your* teen.

Regardless of how quickly you may have arrived at this point, or how unprepared you feel, you have arrived. You are parenting a teen. How strategically and purposefully you approach this next season of parenting will have a huge impact on his or her success in the "real world"—and the quality of your relationship for years to come.

PREPARING FOR LIFE IN THE REAL WORLD

When we contemplated having children, what did most of us think about? Likely our minds were filled with images of babies, toddlers, and elementary school-aged kids. Visions of their first day home, their first steps, their first words, their first ride without training wheels, their first day of school, Little League games, and dance recitals gave us joyful anticipation.

Honestly, few of us pictured a teenager being launched from our loving arms. It's so down the road that it really doesn't enter our minds at the outset. After all, we have SO much time before we get to that point.

Or so it seems.

Then reality hits—and they're off.

If we did think about the teen years, we possibly thought about Friday night football games—maybe our kids or their friends would be football players or cheerleaders or in the band. We might have pictured ourselves helping them with homework and projects. We may have imagined helping them learn to drive and buy their first car, or seeing them off to their senior prom.

Sure, those are important hallmarks of adolescence (in American culture, anyway). But, if those cultural images were as far as our imaginations were able to take us, something was missing.

In our work with educators, youth mentors, and business and community leaders, we are hearing an overwhelming and urgent cry. They tell us the current generation of young adults, generally speaking, is emerging into the world grossly underprepared to succeed. Consider these facts:

» One in four high school students fails to graduate, according to the *Washington Post.*[1]

» In a ranking of 18 industrialized nations, the United States ranked ninth in college enrollment and dead last in college completion.[2]

» The average current teen jobless rate, as of this writing, is 23.7%.[3]

» Over and over we hear that many employers prefer to hire older job applicants, because they are more reliable, better mannered, more motivated, and have a stronger work ethic.

How did we get to this current state of affairs? And what can we parents be doing to equip and empower our teens for *success* in the real world and reverse this course?

AN EMPOWERING APPROACH TO PARENTING

Granted, it's not ALL about us and what we do or don't do. However, the way we train our children does have a great deal of influence on how prepared they are for leaving home and starting life on their own. There are a few approaches to parenting teens that have a significant impact on how well they will fare in life:

1. high expectations, high control style – these can create *strings*
2. low expectations, low control style – these can create *strings*
3. low expectations, high control style –can also create *strings*
4. realistic expectations, empowering style – these can create *wings*

Strings would be anything that would tie our children down and prevent them from achieving their full potential. We *tie our kids down* when we overly control and manage them with a tight grip—even as they mature through the teen years. It can also happen when we coddle, enable, or ignore them. Regardless of which extreme, they are inhibited rather than equipped. Picture a kite—it can never fly free. It is always tied down, constrained, and maneuvered by the person controlling the strings.

Wings are the things we do to prepare our children to be secure, confident, and independent adults, who will live with integrity and impact. We empower our kids when we train them with strong internal guiding principles and give them freedom, opportunity, and accountability to apply those principles according to their unique style and interests. Picture an eagle— it can soar to the heights. It is free to explore high and far and to navigate the turbulence that life often brings.

What does that have to do with parenting? A lot! Here's what strings and wings can look like as we relate to our teens:

STRINGS:
- » *helicoptering* (hovering, reminding, orchestrating, interfering, nagging, meddling)
- » *performance-driven* (excessive pressuring of kids for their achievements and accomplishments, often because of how they reflect on the parent)
- » *vicariousness* (living life through the child; glorying in his or her successes and agonizing in his/her defeats as if they are the parent's own)
- » *enabling* (not letting him/her fail and face consequences; failing to enforce discipline or accountability)
- » *selfishness* (parents thinking it's all about them; taking personally a teen's natural need for space and independence; holding grudges/ outbursts of anger when a teen makes a mistake or makes a decision differently from them; manipulation to get one's own way by withholding rewards or relationship)
- » *overprotection* (being overly fearful of outside influences and

perceived dangers; not allowing kids to experience enough of the real world to make informed choices; restricting them from meeting different people/navigating difficult situations; not permitting them to make their own decisions)

WINGS:
- » *healthy separation* (understanding that teens are their own persons separate from the parents and incrementally giving them space and respect as is due any human)
- » *trust and grace* (giving them incremental freedom *as it is earned* through demonstrating responsibility and integrity; making allowances for immaturity and lack of experience, extending forgiveness and taking the steps needed to re-establish trust when it is broken)
- » *equipping* (strategically and systematically training them to handle real world responsibilities and situations)
- » *empowering* (letting them experience new/different kinds of people and challenging situations with trust and guidance; appreciating their unique design, gifts, and interests and encouraging them accordingly; increasingly having them make their own decisions and supporting them through the consequences)

At a recent educators' conference, a professor from a large Texas university approached me after our workshop on positioning high school students for "real world success." Her question was, "This is great—but how can we get this message to their parents as well?"

She pointed out it's not only teens that are unprepared for the launch—it's parents, too. She pulled out her tablet and opened an email from a student who was failing miserably in math and science. Then, she showed me the most heartbreaking sentence in the girl's email . . . *"I really want to be studying fashion design, but my parents won't let me major in that."*

This young lady had the gifts, creative temperament, and passion for design, but her parents were footing her college bill and had their own expectations and agenda. Unfortunately, everyone involved was suffering—the parents, the daughter, and the university staff and faculty!

Ultimately, raising young adults and releasing them fully prepared for the real world is not supposed to be about *us* (i.e., parents) and our identity, interests, or agenda. It's about doing what's best for *our kids*. It's unfortunate that so many parents have it backwards.

I knew a family whose highly competitive father determined that both of his children would become soccer stars. The 16-year old son spent hours daily practicing drills and maneuvers, at his father's insistence, often turning down outings with his friends to movies, etc.

Though he qualified for international tournaments and awards and enjoyed a great deal of attention for his skills, the boy eventually burnt out. He quit soccer immediately after high school, turning down any advantages his talents might have given him for scholarships or a professional soccer career. When my husband and I ran into him years later, he told us he felt he had lost his childhood, resented his father, and wanted nothing more to do with the sport.

Two classic examples of strings, not wings—both tragic.

STRINGS THAT BREED ENTITLEMENT

What parents don't want their children to follow their dreams, land a solid job, and enjoy a great family life? We want them to be happy. We want them to be well-regarded by others. We want them to be *successful*.

But, here's the rub. In a genuine effort to help our kids be happy and successful, there can be some things we parents do that are extremely counterproductive (as in the scenarios above) and actually work against our objectives. Performance-driven parenting approaches aren't the only ones that do this. Another has commonly become known as "child-centered parenting."

In our work with *What I Wish I Knew at 18*, Dennis and I regularly communicate with teachers and administrators from high schools and universities, as well as employers. They tell us of the growing issues with this younger generation: disrespect for authority, lack of social skills, apathy, and an entitlement mentality. These particular issues squarely stem from the home and are worsening, according to the many organizations working with teens and young adults. The effects of media and culture aren't helping either. Understandably, people in authority positions are concerned.

These effects aren't just happening by accident. It's beyond the scope of this book to comprehensively address them, but we do believe it's our job as parents to do our part and reverse this course. From a parenting perspective, let's consider this scenario:

Two-year old Joey is hungry. Mom says, "Joey, do you want a banana or some grapes?" Joey doesn't want a banana or grapes. Joey wants a mango. Mom tells Joey he needs to eat what is offered to him. He pitches a fit. What does Mom do next? She sends Dad out to the store to buy a mango. Mom and Dad are happy because Joey's happy. Everybody's happy, right? Wrong.

If this style of parenting continues throughout Joey's life, as it does for many, what do you think Joey will grow up thinking? How about:

» he will always have choices
» his happiness and satisfaction should be priorities to the people around him
» he doesn't have to comply with what he is told to do
» Mom will always advocate for him to get his way and come out on top
» other people are there to serve him, not the other way around

This is overly simplistic, but I am trying to make a point. Out of our desire to provide the best for our children (and keep them happy), some of our parenting methods may be contributing to their perception that the world revolves around them. If this is the case, they're in for a rude awakening when they leave home and find that the world owes them nothing. And this is exactly what is happening—in astronomical proportions.

Do you see how this can translate to the business world? To interpersonal skills with professors, coaches, and other superiors? To a marriage? Not very well! Here's what it can look like:

» Parents doing their children's homework, chores, etc.
» Parents defending unacceptable behavior of their children in meetings with school officials
» Parents complaining to and threatening educators, coaches, and employers when their children aren't receiving their desired rewards
» Parents whose lives and schedules are dominated by their children's activities
» Young adults who call in "sick" at the last minute because they've found something better to do
» Young adults who don't take responsibility for their mistakes and shortfalls or show respect to others (especially mature adults)

Entitlement is what we call this attitude, this sense that other people owe us something—that we are deserving, regardless of whether we have done anything to earn it. It stems from the parenting style just described and some undesirable consequences of the "self esteem movement." As a result, children feel *entitled* to get their way, viewing rules as arbitrary and voluntary, their needs as paramount, and other people as existing to serve them. And parents, usually unwittingly, are the ones who are cultivating this mindset.

In order for parents to give our young adults wings on which they can *really fly*, we can't coddle them. If we've been doing it up to this point (as revealed in our children's' behavior), it needs to be addressed before they get out into the real world.

We can't set our kids up as the center of our universe and let them think the planets revolve around them. It may seem a short-term solution when they're pitching a fit as a two-year old, or even as an immature teenager. But in the long run, it will come back to bite us—and them.

GIVING THEM WINGS IN THE REAL WORLD

It's not easy raising teenagers, especially in our cultural climate that sends so many mixed messages (many destructive), offers innumerable distractions, and poses any number of potential perils for young people.

These days, some parents are parenting out of fear and struggling with their children's need for independence. Others think, "My kid's not ready to run his own life. If we let go, he'll blow it." Some on the other end of the spectrum think, "It's not my job to teach her how to be successful; that's the school's job!"

The fact is, whether you fall off a horse on one side or the other doesn't matter; you've still fallen off the horse. It *is* our job as parents to train and release our children successfully into the real world—and to empower them to live confidently and independently, with integrity and impact. It's not as intimidating as it might sound. And it's not rocket science. You can do it, and you can do it well.

Yes, parenting is a challenge. That's because it is a whole-person endeavor. You are needed for so much more than simply providing food, clothes, shelter, and a ride to practice. You are developing a person—mind, body, and spirit. That may not be what you signed up for—but it's the role you are in. You are uniquely equipped to parent *your* children, whether they are yours by birth, adoption, foster care, or step-parenting. Perhaps you are a grandparent stepping into the "parent" role. No matter what your situation, you DO have what it takes to set them up for success and let them go with confidence—to give them wings, not strings.

Are you ready to release an eagle to soar?

TAKE FIVE

There are two lasting bequests we can give our children.
One is roots. The other is wings.
Hodding Carter, Jr.

By the time children reach the teen years and parents need to start letting go, confidence and trust should be every mother and father's goal. Time and experience should prove that we are raising—and releasing—mature, trustworthy, well-adjusted, honest, and motivated young adults who are ready to tackle the world and make an impact.

Think about where you are right now in your parenting process, as it relates to the inevitable "launch." How would you answer the following questions?

» Are we thinking ahead to the transition and how we are going to approach it?

» Are we setting goals and making decisions for our teens based on *our* interests and aspirations, or based on *theirs*?

» When we look at the lists of characteristics describing "wings" versus "strings" where do we see ourselves? Do we need to be prepared to make some adjustments to our parenting style? In what areas?

» What inspires us about the idea of giving our teens "wings" instead of "strings?" What concerns us and why?

CHAPTER TWO

KEEP YOUR EYES ON THE GOAL

*If you don't know where you are going,
you will probably end up somewhere else.*
Lawrence J. Peter

"Caution: Some Assembly Required!" We've all seen these warnings countless times and for many, it's no big deal. On the other hand, for those of us mechanically challenged, it sends us into the *Land of Pain*.

I (Dennis) vividly recall assembling a swing set and following the directions to a T. Through concentration, toil, and sweat, I did it! Or, so I thought. Afterwards, I noticed there were a few seemingly important parts left over—never a good sign. It was clear I had built a swing with accidents just waiting to happen.

I took a break and, after composing myself, reread the instructions from start to finish. A third of the way through, I realized the problem. The manufacturer forgot to include some needed steps in the instructions! Bewildered, I did my best to invent them, and eventually our son, Michael, was in his little slice of heaven. There was one other problem with these instructions. They were totally lacking in visual images of each step and the final product. How was I supposed to know whether I was properly assembling the thing? It was blind faith at its worst.

Through the years, I've built many things, some which went smoothly and others not so well. The common denominator to the easy ones was having images of a proper assembly—lots of images. The endgame. The goal. The prize!

In Stephen Covey vernacular, we call this "beginning with the end in mind." It means having clearly described goals for our projects and for our lives. Goals that, by their mere presence, offer inspiration, motivation, and focus. Goals that are aspirational but achievable, and above all else, worthy. Goals that, once achieved, will instill pride in a job well done.

So it goes with preparing children for adulthood, doesn't it? After all, they enter this world prewired and prepackaged with parts that will require some guided assembly by their caregivers. Will we train with lots of little instructions, but lack the "big picture" vision to lead us along the way? Or, will we be strategic and purposeful, giving our children and our relationship the best chances for success?

Wouldn't it help to have a well-defined endgame for our parenting?

TAKING ON AN INTENTIONAL MINDSET

From as far back as I can remember, I looked forward to becoming a dad. When I was young, I could regularly be found on the driveway or ball field coaching the neighborhood children like a modern-day Pied Piper. I figured that a love for children was the main ingredient to being a great dad and didn't really think much beyond that. Besides, it would be that much easier if they were your own, wouldn't it? You know, like the Harry Chapin line from *Cat's in the Cradle*, " . . . the boy was just like me."

And, then along came Michael—our 9 lbs., 7 oz. bundle of joy and energy. And energy. And energy. Oh, did I say, "energy?" He had my dimple and dark hair, so we were on our way. Cute kid, too!

We would arrive home from the hospital and he, Jeanne, and I would begin our new life as a threesome. So far, so good. That was until three hours later when the thermometer indicated a temperature of 105! Needless to say, it was panic city, and my feelings of "This is a piece of cake" were soon replaced with "I'm so over my head!" A little voice was telling me that maybe this dad thing wasn't as easy as I thought it would be. And, truth be told, it wasn't. But looking back now, I wouldn't trade it for anything in the world.

What have I learned in 23+ years of fathering, as of this writing? A lot! For one, it requires far more than a fanciful imagination of what parenting is all about. Effective parenting of teens requires an intentional mindset deserving of this vital role, including:

1. Understanding and accepting the responsibility that comes with parenting
Great parenting isn't just about having fun or keeping our children happy. It's not that fun isn't a part of it, but that's the sideshow to the main event. It means we are primarily responsible for loving, nurturing, training, affirming, supporting, and empowering our children to be independent and responsible adults. It's not about being their friend (as many TV shows would lead you to believe). Rather, it's about helping them develop their leadership qualities and preparing them for life and the key decisions awaiting them. It means having the courage to show tough love when behavioral modification is needed, even if it means not being liked for a period of time.

2. Having agreement on the parenting team
It is crucial that parents and guardians be on the same page when it comes to goals, attitudes, and methods. Think of it as *one team, one dream!* To that end, it helps to review and discuss some of the excellent parenting resources out there, along with your own parenting background (how you were parented) and observations of other families you may want to emulate (or not).

Understanding and agreeing on our parenting responsibilities is a team effort where each partner needs to support, encourage, and reinforce the other. To do otherwise will lead to fireworks and to children who will manipulate the "weaker party" on an issue.

If you and your child's other parent are not together, you can still have a unified front on parenting methods, for the sake of the children. Try to put aside any other differences and find places of agreement on your parenting goals.

3. Remembering you're not just raising children—you're raising future adults
In this age of busyness, it's easy to get consumed with the day-to-day tasks and logistics. It's also easy to focus on each micro-phase of development as children migrate from one grade and stage to the next. While some of this is clearly understandable and valuable, it's always helpful to remember you're raising future adults—that's the endgame.

What habits, behaviors, and attitudes are being formed today that will need correcting down the road? What praises and recognition can be given for demonstrating responsibility beyond their years? It pays to start early in the process, so fewer corrections will be required in the later teen years, closer to the launch, when they're exerting their independence.

4. Recognizing it's not about you
Jeanne and I are athletic, detail-oriented MBAs, who are stable in temperament and lack a creative bone in our bodies. So, wouldn't it stand to reason that Michael would be a blend of these attributes? Ha! We soon learned that his gifts, interests, and temperament were not from *our* gene pool. We gave birth to a delightfully creative kid who was nothing like his parents. Not better. Not worse. Just different. And, we (gladly) learned to work with that.

Unfortunately, we see a growing trend of parents putting pressure on their children to be just like them—or, just like someone else, such as their more successful friend or their smarter or more athletic sibling. Although, usually unwittingly, these parents are striving for performance or replication, rather than parenting, to bring out the best in their uniquely designed children. They're defining their own esteem and worth by how well their children perform. The result is children who feel unloved and never good enough.

Most parents are not doing this intentionally. It's natural for us to want our children to perform at their best, and it's always nice when we share similar interests. However, it's easy to overdo it if we're not careful. Where we really see the fallout is when they enter the teen years.

LOOKING AHEAD TO THE LAUNCH

By keeping these points and our goals in mind, we'll enjoy a smoother ride with more reliable outcomes. After all, goals foster greater focus, motivation, and accountability, don't they?

When forming our parenting goals, it helps to remember the three critical components to a successful launch into adulthood: 1) the destination, 2) our relationship/support structure, and 3) the transition. Each is essential, and they're meant to work together in harmony:

First is the all-important *destination*. In reality, there are many milestones as we parent our children: things like successful potty training, tying their own shoes, the first day of kindergarten, their first report card, sports and rehearsals, middle school, their first date, their driver's license, their first job, college and career planning, and culminating with their high school graduation. With each milestone marker, time passes more quickly and, as any parent of a high school graduate will attest, in retrospect it's like the blink of an eye.

Our "destination," in this case, is the milestone launch into adulthood and the knowledge our children will require to do it successfully. This involves:

1. covering the bases with the *wisdom* our children need for "real world" independence (i.e., what do they need to know?)
2. instilling the *principles* and values for honorable living (i.e., how should they live?)
3. helping our children discover their *unique* assets they bring to the world (i.e., "who am I, what do I have to offer, and what are my opportunities?")

Together, these goals define holistic preparation for a healthy and fulfilling life.

Next involves building an enduring *relationship/support structure* based on love, trust, and mutual understanding. As parents, it is our responsibility to guide, affirm, correct, encourage, and support our children as they develop into tomorrow's adults. This requires open channels of communication, where all parties feel safe to share and open to receive each other's perspectives. Naturally, it becomes more challenging during the teenage years when children are increasingly exerting their independence. Mom and Dad aren't quite as smart as they used to be, even though the same words, uttered by their friends' parents, seem to carry their weight in gold!

We will have something to say about relationships in the chapters ahead, but, suffice it to say, an effective parenting approach needs to evolve from "control" to "influence." For many, if not most of us, this can be a very difficult transition. But, it's a transition that must be made in order to prepare them for independence and for your relationship to thrive and endure.

There are many ingredients to a successful parenting relationship, but two stand out as especially important at this time of life—*unconditional love* and your *belief* in your children. Teens and young adults face enormous transitions and pressure as they accept new responsibilities and adjust to new environments. They will make their share of mistakes along the way, and having the benefit of unconditional love from their parents and support structure is a huge blessing—a safety net they can always count on.

Related, it is a tremendous asset for teens to have parents who believe in them. That belief is an inner voice encouraging kids to dream big and persevere through life's challenges. It is a gift that will keep giving for a lifetime. After all, your belief will breed their belief. That's huge!

Finally, the last component to a successful launch involves preparing for the all-important *transition*. Regardless of whether our children are headed to college, career, or military service, the first six to nine months after graduation are critical. It is during this brief time that many young people derail, unable to adjust well to their new life chapter. The loneliness that comes from losing their convenient support structure can be overwhelming. The recognition that "life will never be the same" hits some much harder than others.

The more our children are prepared for the variety of feelings and their new responsibilities during this season, the better equipped they will be for a successful transition. In the obstacle course called "life," there's nothing like getting off to a strong start!

WHAT ARE *YOUR* PARENTING GOALS?

It might be helpful at this point to pause and identify exactly what your own endgame is when it comes to raising and releasing your children into the real world. To do so, you are going to need to take some things into consideration, such as your own upbringing and expectations, those of your spouse, and the aptitudes and aspirations of your teens.

I was the youngest of four children and the first in my family to attend college. If you had asked my parents when I was young if that was their *goal* for me, they probably would have said "no," since that wasn't a part of their own experience. Now, having the benefit of a college education myself, I see the value in it and we made it a goal for Michael and Lauren. This goal shaped how Jeanne and I spoke to them, the expectations we had of their schoolwork, and the way we planned financially. Do you see how one's background and perspective can make a difference?

Your goals for your teen should be achievable, measurable, and identifiable without being directional (meaning, we don't want to set a goal that our child will be a doctor, which would be directional. That's his or her choice, not ours.) Goals should include intrinsic, as well as extrinsic qualities.

For example, the goals that your teen will leave home able to do his own laundry, balance a checking account, and cook at least simple meals would be extrinsic qualities. Intrinsic goals would be character qualities you want to see cultivated in your teen, such as integrity, honesty, faith, good stewardship, diligence, respect, and so on.

Following is a list of sample goals. Feel free to add your own and cross off those that don't apply to you. You and your spouse should go through the lists together. Which items are the same? Which are different? You will want to come to agreement (or at least compromise) on these.

Possible goals	Not important	Somewhat important	Very important
EXTRINSIC			
Finish high school			
Minimum 3.6 GPA			
Participate in HS sports/clubs			
Participate in faith community			
College education			
Trade or technical education			
Fulfilling career			
Financial literacy			
Skills for keeping/maintaining house			
Healthy eating/cooking habits			
Effective time management			
Strong family			
Other . . .			
INTRINSIC			
Honesty, truthfulness			
Respect			
Compassion, kindness			
Service-minded			
Faith			
Self-control			
Self-discipline			
Diligence, work ethic			
Maturity			
Leadership			
Team player			
Other . . .			

This exercise helps to define goals to be reinforced and affirmed along the way. It is valuable to develop and discuss them together with your teen, as he or she becomes more independent.

A *PARENTING* MISSION STATEMENT?

Any successful organization has a guiding mission statement that describes its purpose and objectives. It's an aspiring vision for the future, together with the underlying core values or desired outcomes that drive its strategy and practices. Most companies put a great deal of effort into developing a mission statement because it defines the organization and frames its goals. It's something every employee is expected to uphold.

Should we consider taking a page from the business playbook and develop a mission statement to guide our parenting? Our families? I think so!

In an essay adapted from his book, *The Secrets of Happy Families: Improve Your Mornings, Rethink Family Dinner, Fight Smarter, Go Out and Play, and Much More*, Bruce Feiler shares the merits of a Family Mission Statement. Family members participate in articulating their mission and purpose, and core values and principles. It's a way to define the family's "brand" and serves as an identity statement and set of guiding behaviors and attitudes.

When developing the statement, families mutually agree on roles and accountabilities, and children are free to offer constructive feedback to their parents. They have weekly "roundtable" meetings to review the prior week (how did we do and what can we do better next time?) and determine plans, goals, and workload allocations for the next. They work together to make and enforce daily checklists (with flexibility to accommodate the unexpected) and resolve conflicts in predetermined ways with less stress and fireworks. It's proactive rather than reactive. It's empowering. There's less nagging too, and kids seem to like it!

Many organizations develop separate mission and vision statements. However, because parenting has such a developmental aspect to it, there's merit to combining them. Let's consider the possibilities by first defining the components:

» The *mission*—our overarching purpose and objective. It captures what we do, for whom, and for what benefit.

» The *vision*—our inspirational and aspiring goals for the future (where we want to go and why) that are realistic and achievable.

» The *core values* and expected *outcomes*—our unwavering, guiding principles that govern our behavior, decisions, and attitudes. They can also include expected outcomes from successfully implementing our mission and vision.

Mission statements can be developed at the family level, parent unit, or individually. When applied to the family or parent units, it is critical that each member has a voice in the final product. Your kids will enjoy and appreciate being involved in the process and will feel a sense of ownership to abide by the terms. Remember, it's one team, one dream!

TRY THIS:

A PARENTING MISSION STATEMENT

What follows is a hypothetical parenting mission statement. Consider developing your own as you raise your future adult. This bit of strategic parenting will take some effort, but can pay huge dividends in the long run.

MISSION

To inspire, equip, and empower our future adults who are admired for their character, respected for their gifts and talents, and remembered for the love and service they gave to others.

VISION

We will raise future leaders of excellence who will live purposefully and honorably, who will understand and passionately offer their unique assets, who will leave a legacy of significance and joyful service, who will value relationships and faith, who will exude gratitude and courage, and who will live with the confidence of knowing they are loved unconditionally and believed-in emphatically.

CORE VALUES

1. We will assume primary responsibility and accountability for developing, nurturing, and supporting our children to become well-prepared, honorable, and productive leaders.
2. We accept the responsibility of serving as the chief role models for our children and practice what we teach.
3. We will parent as a team, complementing, advising, and affirming each other in a spirit of love and cooperation.
4. We will demonstrate unequivocally through our actions, words, and attitudes that our children are loved unconditionally.
5. We will actively seek to build strong relationships and communicate based on love, trust, respect, active listening, and mutual understanding.
6. We will support self-discovery in our children to facilitate a comprehensive understanding of their unique design, assets, and opportunities.
7. We will help our children build a personal leadership foundation for life that fosters wise decision-making.
8. We will honor our children's uniqueness and empower them to live their dreams.
9. We will actively engage loving adults in the lives of our children.
10. We will value their person more than their performance and regularly communicate our belief in them.

This is just an example, based on our parenting goals as our kids were growing up. Now, see what you can come up with for your own family.

Remember, it's never too early to begin "parenting for adulthood." At the same time, it's never too late! However, the sooner we begin, the sooner we will help build the leadership foundation our children need for life. By keeping our eyes on the goal, we'll improve our parenting and ultimately, their destination.

With our goals understood and articulated, let's turn to building a strong leadership foundation in your teen that will set him or her up for a lifetime of success.

TAKE FIVE

When it comes to our parenting, it pays to begin with the end in mind. With that, consider the following questions:

1. What are your goals for your children? How would your goals compare to their own?
2. What are your core values as a family? How would you describe your family's "brand?"
3. How might the concept of "raising future adults" rather than "raising children" change your way of thinking?
4. How might you develop and apply the concept of a parenting or family mission statement for your household?

CHAPTER THREE

BUILD A SOLID LEADERSHIP FOUNDATION

Leadership is action, not position.
Donald H. McGannon

"So, Dad, did *you* earn a 4.0?"

It was a Sunday night in August 2008 and my conscience paid an unexpected visit. Alone in my bedroom and ready to wind down for the evening, I (Dennis) was caught off-guard by the most convicting parenting moment of my life. I began reflecting on the fact that I'd had my son for 17 years and we were down to two weeks before the "big launch." Michael would soon be off to Pepperdine University and entering the "real world" on his own.

Being the consummate analytic, my mind was bombarded by one thought after another. "Have I covered all the bases?" "What conversations do we need before our send-off? "How well have I prepared him for independent life?" "What is my parenting GPA?" Frankly, it hit me like a ton of bricks.

In a moment of resolve, I went to my den, opened up a Word document on my computer, and began to write. In what seemed like no time, I recorded a list of "life success pointers" for Michael, based on the incredible leaders I've known and researched in my career, service, and personal life arenas. The phrases of wisdom ranged from personal leadership attributes to the key life-decisions Michael would be making in the years ahead. Over 100 pointers came to me in one sitting that night—a surreal experience, to say the least. (We have included these success pointers for you on page 193 in Appendix B of this book.)

The next morning, it became apparent to me this list was meant for more than a few last minute father/son conversations. I knew I wasn't the only parent in the same boat. Surely, I would have been a better father had I had this "destination guide" from the get-go! So, at the urging of many of my friends and mentors, my "encore career" as author, publisher, mentor, and educator was born. I began writing my first book, *What I Wish I Knew at 18: Life Lessons for the Road Ahead* and started a publishing business. Never in my wildest dreams . . .

While most parents experiencing their first-time launch don't write a book or change careers because of it, sending a child off into the "real world" is a huge milestone and certainly a defining moment. How well we prepare our children for independent life is one of our ultimate tests.

DID we earn a 4.0?

WE KNOW WE'VE GOT PROBLEMS— HOW ABOUT SOLUTIONS?

I guess I figured it would be easier. Surely, with the plethora of parenting books out there, I would have no problem finding the perfect **destination guide**—you know, the "end" of "begin with the end in mind." I wish it were that simple. Most books I found seemed to focus on the relational and behavioral aspects of parenting.

What about parenting support groups? I didn't find much in that department, either. It seems most major parenting groups are focused on the little ones. (Maybe parents of teens just don't want to talk about it?)

Well, there's always school! Surely, our educators will teach my kids to become well-prepared leaders of integrity, ready to tackle life's big decisions involving career, family, and finances. You know, training the whole person and not just the mind? Think again. Many if not most schools are focused on the core subjects that satisfy the college admission requirements. After all, Trigonometry is more important to life than Personal Finance, isn't it?

What about schools promoting character, leadership, productivity, and life skills?

"Well, that's really the domain of parents, but perhaps we can offer an elective, if we can fit it into our budget."

How about good old fashioned, on-the-job training? There was a time when jobs for teens were commonplace. I was a grocery store stock boy and could have also pumped gas if I wanted. Nowadays, with the regulatory environment as it is and many ideal jobs filled with white-haired people who held too much stock in their 401Ks, teen unemployment is somewhere in the stratosphere. So much for opportunities to acquire "real world" life skills and witnessing firsthand that life isn't always fair.

Well, there's always culture. After all, it's the information age! Surely, our kids can acquire some life-smarts and values from the media and entertainment industry, can't they? It goes without saying that most programming isn't exactly modeling what employers are looking for. For example, there's a new show out called *Pregnant & Dating*. How's that for role modeling? The (negative) cultural forces are powerful and becoming increasingly juvenile and destructive with each new season. This only adds to our dilemma.

With all that in mind, is it any wonder so many employers are aghast at the lack of preparedness found in many young adults and the amount of retraining required? A senior executive of a large national corporation told me that one recent job applicant brought his mother to his final interview? Seriously!

In my lifetime, our society has progressed positively in so many ways. However, in terms of life preparedness for our younger generation, I believe we've distinctly *regressed*. From family instability to educational priorities to meager employment opportunities to warped cultural messages, our teens aren't receiving the best foundation possible for establishing a healthy, productive and successful life. And, it's showing in many of the statistics we see in the news every day.

It's hard to overestimate the importance of developing a strong foundation in our children. At its core, this should include developing a platform for personal leadership and effective life decision-making skills. It means offering a strategic vision for life based on *universal values* and the practices of *admired leaders*. And, it means covering the bases with principles that define great outcomes—principles that will:

» sustain them during life's ups and downs

» bring out their "inner leader" in terms of attitudes, behaviors, and decisions

» remain strong when their values are challenged and when adversity strikes

» provide before-the-fact wisdom so they make key decisions *right the first time*

» encourage them to think strategically and purposefully about life

» offer a comprehensive picture of who they are, what they uniquely have to offer, and what their opportunities are

» inspire and empower them to use all they've got to live their dreams and positively impact the world

DEVELOPING A FOUNDATION FOR LIFE

Consider this real life scenario: the Human Resources Department sifted through countless applications before narrowing the field to five finalists. Having done its homework, the hiring team was anxious to fill the position and get on with it. They knew it would be a tough call because the applications were so strong.

One could only imagine how nervous the candidates would be on the eve of their interviews. This job market was painful, and they finally had a decent shot. Each was convinced that he or she would win the prize.

Much to the employer's surprise, the decision was easy. One candidate clearly stood out from the pack. Can you guess which one it was? It was the only one who showed up on time!

This story is becoming all-too-common these days where a sense of entitlement and a lack of self-discipline have taken hold of many young people. In a world this competitive, it's hard to fathom. What's the common denominator of the four who lost? They all lacked a personal leadership foundation—and for it they paid a dear price.

Helping teens develop a leadership foundation for life is one of our most important parenting responsibilities. It has a huge bearing on whether they will reach their full potential and make wise life-decisions. A successful leadership foundation has five key characteristics:

>> *Comprehensive*—it must encompass the key aspects of life and our most important decisions
>> *Personal*—it is unique to each individual and involves body, mind, and spirit
>> *Principled*—it must be grounded in universal truths, honor, and wisdom
>> *Practical*—it must be "real-world relevant" and not simply theoretical
>> *Enduring*—it must stand the test of time and survive life's challenges

In the following section, we describe the six pillars of the foundation young adults need for a successful, healthy, and fulfilling life. (Appendix A provides an overview diagram.) Let's overview each foundational pillar, along with critical preparation questions for parents to consider. Each pillar is an essential component to the overall foundation and deserves our best nurturing. (Note: more detail on these concepts, messaged directly to teens, can be found in chapters one through six of my book *What I Wish I Knew at 18: Life Lessons for the Road Ahead*.)

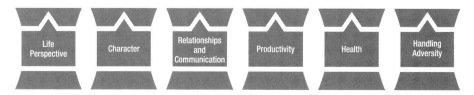

🏛 LIFE PERSPECTIVE

A successful life begins with a healthy perspective of life. Our most profound questions (e.g., who am I, what do I have to offer, what are my opportunities, and what will be my legacy?) demand a measure of seriousness atypical of most teenagers. It's up to us to help plant these seeds by promoting and guiding their self-discovery.

At the core of a healthy perspective is an understanding of our **worth** and value. (We will devote an entire chapter to this later, because it's that critical.) Destructive choices, such as substance abuse, crime, gang affiliation, dropping out of school, teen pregnancy, and suicide derive from a sense of worthlessness and hopelessness about life. Teens need to know they are unconditionally loved and come to understand their unique value and assets. Parents have to take the lead role in this, using every opportunity to reveal these special qualities and gifts to their children.

Related, our life has **purpose**. We are either born with, or develop, passions to use our talents in productive, impactful ways. Parents have a special opportunity to help their children identify what brings them joy, fulfillment, and inspiration. Understanding our talents and showing the different ways they can be used is an inspirational and motivational gift we can all give our children.

Another key ingredient to a healthy life perspective is having a worthy **definition of "success."** Our culture drivers work overtime to send messages that "success" is about money, fame, power, beauty, and the like. Sometimes it seems an impossible message to counteract, but fight it we must! The fact is, how we define success will govern how we live our lives. It's that fundamental.

I propose a more worthy definition of success: how well we loved, how we used our talents to make the world a better place, the character we modeled, the priorities we set, and whether we gave it our best. Help your children develop a true meaning of "success" and you will give them a legacy gift.

The center of our **life focus** is yet another important aspect of our perspective. Are we living for self or for others? (For people of faith, the question will also include how we are living for God.) Many "me-oriented" people eventually see the emptiness of a self-centered approach, so the younger we can instill other-centeredness in our children the better. There is no better way than involving them in service that helps people less fortunate. You might also invite your children into your charitable giving decisions. Jeanne and I did this with our kids (and still do) and it's been extremely rewarding for all of us. It's a great way to instill service-mindedness and to see which causes they're passionate about.

Developing a **positive outlook** on life is another hallmark of building a strong foundation. Our mindset informs our leadership abilities, our relationships, our motivation, and our ability to handle adversity. We can't always be happy, but a positive outlook makes all the difference in the world. The most revered people have an uncanny ability to lift people up because of their natural positivity.

Successful people also take a **strategic view** to life, understanding that some decisions can have long-term consequences. They consciously avoid potentially destructive situations because their future is worth more than the risk. In order to fulfill one's purpose, it's important we take a long-term view of life.

Did you notice how each of these components to a healthy life-perspective requires that our children feel *secure*? The more insecure the child, the more he or she is me-oriented, negative, aimless, and prone to superficial definitions of success. A secure child is a hopeful and purposeful adult in the making!

Here are some questions to help build a healthy, strategic life-perspective in your children:

» Do they understand their unique gifts, talents, passions, and worth?
» Do they know how to live strategically with discipline and purpose?
» Are they focused on others before themselves?
» Are they guided by a worthy definition of success?
» Are they confident enough to take risks, even if they may not succeed?

» Do they project a positive attitude and recognize that life isn't always fair?

» Do they consider the long-term consequences of key decisions and choices?

» Are they adaptable to changing circumstances?

» Are they about empowerment or entitlement?

Your teens will be facing many new decisions (and potentially compromising situations) soon after they leave home, and their view of life and their future will play a huge role in how they respond. Helping your children develop a strong perspective should be one of your most important priorities.

▓ CHARACTER

Benjamin Franklin is credited with the saying that the only things certain in life are death and taxes. Allow me to add a third—the certainty that when your teen leaves home, his or her values will be tested! How will he or she hold up, especially when homesick, "friendsick," or experiencing a raging case of the "lonelies?" During times like these, it helps mightily to have a strong character foundation. It also pays to have a well-developed list of *non-negotiable* values that they will, under no circumstances, compromise!

On page 146 you will find a list of values to discuss with your teen. Additionally, here are some helpful pointers to reinforce:

» Character is modeled through our attitudes, behaviors, and decisions, and is often revealed by what you do when no one else is looking.

» It is extremely difficult to recover from a damaged reputation.

» Surround yourself with positive people who will help uphold your values, not encourage you to compromise them.

» The best way to maintain strong character is to avoid potentially compromising situations. The old adage, "an ounce of prevention is worth a pound of cure" applies!

» You may not always *feel* loved or even liked by other people, but you *must* be trusted.

» Don't say something about someone else you'd regret if they heard (hard to do, but such a great discipline).

» If you're not sure whether to do or say something, imagine it as the headline in tomorrow's newspaper.

As you develop a strong character foundation in your teens, here are some helpful questions to consider:

» Are they guided by integrity in everything?

» Do they demonstrate love, kindness, and respect toward others?

» Do they live with honor and self-discipline?

» Do they stand up for their beliefs and values with conviction?

» Are they people of humility who encourage others?

» Do they demonstrate a commitment to excellence and giving it their best effort?

» Do they take full responsibility for their mistakes and shortfalls?

» Do they embrace constructive feedback?

» Are their communications honorable about others who are not present?

In the "pressure cooker" teen and young adult years when they're facing major life transitions and social adjustments, they will slip up. That's one reason it's so important to share in humility your own mistakes, so they know you weren't perfect either.

RELATIONSHIPS AND COMMUNICATION

I think I realized that life was about relationships when I first set foot on the campus of the University of Wisconsin-Eau Claire. I grew up in a smallish village in Wisconsin, where I knew everyone and they all knew me. Most of my relatives lived close by, too. I lived in the same little house in the same neighborhood throughout my school years and made many friends along the way. Life was easy and secure.

After my parents dropped me off that day, I quickly realized my life would never be the same. Now, my future would be more influenced by the new people I would meet. Most of my friends had scattered to other colleges, and my family was now a six-hour drive or a three-dollar per minute long distance call away. On a campus of 12,000, I knew only three and felt like the letter "D" in a bowl of alphabet soup. My only consolation was that everyone else was in the same boat, trying to figure it out just like me.

And now, even in our connected world of mobile phones, Facebook and Skype, it *still* isn't easy.

That's why it's imperative that we help develop strong relational skills in our teens to prepare them for this major adjustment and new reality. Their happiness and success, both personally and professionally, will be heavily influenced by their relationships and communications with others. Consider the host of new relational spheres they'll be experiencing in coming years:

» College—fellow students and faculty
» Career—supervisors, peers, subordinates, clients, prospects, service providers
» Friends—preserving long-term relationships and building new ones
» Love—a potential spouse along with his/her family
» Community—service and recreational organizations
» Places of worship
» A family of their own

Clearly, many new relationships will be formed! And, as we become a more mobile workforce with shorter career stints, that means more relocations, more transitions, and more relationships to build. "Starting over" is rapidly becoming the new normal.

Frankly, some of us handle this better than others. The first transitions after leaving home and when we enter the workforce can be brutal. With that in mind, here are some key skills that will help your teen immensely:

» Meeting new people with confidence and making a great first impression

» Developing friendships patiently with people who share their values and interests

» Understanding that everyone isn't meant to be their friend and if they have to compromise their values to be someone's "friend," the friendship is not worth it

» Demonstrating strong listening skills (i.e., more ears, less mouth!)

» Being a positive and encouraging team player who can disagree respectfully

» Having the ability to confidently *engage* in conversation using proper respect and manners

» Being able to accurately read the non-verbal cues of others

» Demonstrating an ability to express feelings and emotions, in healthy ways

While these offer some good training fodder, here are some additional questions for you to consider when helping your children build a solid relational foundation:

» Do they prioritize relationships over things?

» How well do they engage in *meaningful* conversations in an increasingly superficial, technological world?

» How easy is it for them to show appreciation and gratitude toward others?

» Do they understand that, when working in teams, it's not a question of *who* is right, but what is right?

PRODUCTIVITY

I've noticed an interesting trend in my chance encounters with people. It goes something like this:

Me: "It's great to see you! How've you been?"
Them: "Busy!" Or,
Them: "Crazy busy!" Or,
Them: "Out of control!" Or,
Them: "Overwhelmed!"

Is this good?

No, it's not. We're experiencing a crisis of over-commitment and information overload like never before. It's not supposed to be this way. After all, technology is supposed to make us more efficient, isn't it? At the risk of sounding like Fred Flintstone, faster isn't always better—especially if it reduces our quality of life and productivity!

These days, everyone is consumed with "busyness." You see it everywhere. Our attention spans are shorter (did any Smartphone providers warn us of that?), our responsiveness has markedly deteriorated, our cell phones have become appendages (where almost nonstop beeps and vibrations are creating a false sense of urgency), we're having a harder time focusing, and relational depth is increasingly being replaced by superficial breadth. Our children are bombarded with information and opportunities like never before. We have to arm them with a strong productivity foundation to handle this brave new world.

Let's start with time management. Whether they go on to college or the workplace, they will be in charge of how they spend their time. Successful people are extremely disciplined with their time, viewing it as a priceless asset they cannot get back. That's the attitude we want to cultivate in our teens. They will need to develop prioritized "to-do lists" arranged by importance and urgency, and plan their time accordingly. (I find it key to block my time in 30-minute intervals and avoid allowing lower-level interruptions and distractions to interfere. Once the key priorities are accomplished, then it's okay to have dessert!)

Another key productivity driver is their ability to set goals and plan for their achievement. Encourage your children to set goals regarding their career, family, education, finances, service, experiences, recreation/leisure, and daily responsibilities. The more specific, realistic, and measurable they are, the better. And, when it comes to workplace projects, it pays to plan for completion at least a day before the due date and to work backwards to meet the interim deadlines.

Finally, our kids need to become great decision makers. In *What I Wish I Knew at 18*, I describe an effective six-step decision-making process. The steps are: 1) determine your key decision criteria, 2) get the facts, 3) identify all the alternatives, 4) conduct an objective pro/con analysis for each option, 5) engage wise counsel, and 6) listen to your "gut instinct" or intuition. By working the process, their best option will usually reveal itself.

Here are some questions to consider as you "parent for productivity":

» Are they effective goal setters, planners, time managers, and decision-makers?

» Do they control technology, rather than allow technology to control them?

» In their daily planning, do they focus first on what matters most?

» Do they consider their time as a precious asset?

⬛ HEALTH

What's the one thing we often take for granted until we lose it? I know for me it's health. And yet, our ability to be at our best is dependent on having a well-functioning body, mind, and spirit! That's why our health is another leadership foundation pillar we need to build in our children.

In many respects, this pillar is more about our children *just doing it* rather than knowing what to do. It is the one pillar that is a required course in school, and it is a rare day when parents don't have something to say about it. However, it's one thing to be dependent on parents for your well-being and quite another to be on your own, practicing all those good habits they've instilled!

Most of us are familiar with the "Freshman 15" (the average pound-age gained in the first year of college!), and I doubt I was any different.

Desserts were unlimited, and I vividly recall storing Fudgsicles® in the sliding window of my dorm room during those harsh Wisconsin winters. Oh, and did I mention pizza? Lots and lots of pizza!

It is outside the scope of this book to offer a comprehensive primer on health, but here are some key areas to cover:

» Physical—nutrition, personal hygiene, exercise, rest and relaxation, personal safety, medical examinations, and high-risk behavior (e.g., substance abuse)

» Mental—emotional, behavioral, learning/intelligence, decision-making/critical thinking, judgment, and stress management

» Spiritual—faith, perseverance/handling adversity, moral/ethical compass, worth, reflection, eternal questions, forgiveness, and for people of faith: worship, fellowship, and prayer

As parents, it is our responsibility to nurture the "whole person" for independent life. Many young people are failing to learn key life skills, because parents and schools think the *other* is covering the bases. Our kids are the unintended victims of these faulty assumptions.

Here are some helpful questions for parents to consider when building a strong pillar of health:

» How well have you covered the physical, mental, and spiritual bases described above as you envision your teen as a soon-to-be-independent adult?

» Which areas do your teen or young adult feel least secure about, whether involving knowledge or principles? How would you evaluate your teen in terms of body, mind, and spiritual health, and what actions are you prepared to take to address any areas of concern?

» What aspects of health training are being covered in school and what key principles are they teaching? You might be surprised!

▓ HANDLING ADVERSITY

Sometimes life hands us a lemon. The question is, what do we do about it when it's our turn?

Adversity comes in so many forms and on its own mysterious time-table. It can involve personal loss, disappointments, mistakes, bad luck, or mistreatment. Some experience it earlier in life than others. For some it's highly episodic, while for others it can be a daily reality. Sometimes our adversity is the result of our own actions, while most of the time it's not our fault. This is why we all react to our adversity so differently.

Life's unexpected road bumps touch us in a variety of ways, some of which will be new territory for a young adult. They can involve college academics, career decisions, relationships, health, finances, a death in the family, or simply dealing with profound disappointment in the way things are going. In my case, it was an unexpectedly bad college academic transition and being on the receiving end of a breakup with my three-year college girlfriend. Talk about taking the wind out of my sails!

To young people launching into adulthood, handling adversity can be especially tough. For one thing, they may not have the support structure of family and friends nearby to help them through it. Also, just as they are trying to discover and prove themselves as adults, adversity can strike from their own choices and mistakes. After all, the more independent we are, the more chances we have to mess up! Adversity can be an easier pill to swallow when it isn't our fault.

Developing a strong adversity pillar is another important parenting priority. Even if the other pillars are rock solid, an inability to persevere through life's challenges can destroy the foundation. Parents can play a huge preventive role by offering the reassurance that adversity happens to everyone, nobody's perfect, we often grow from it, and the real question is how we deal with it when it happens.

Don't let their adversity today develop into a fear of failure. It's essential to help them stay hopeful and recognize that pain has a way of subsiding, just like it does when we cut our finger. Show them their current low is not their new normal. There's nothing worse than today's adversity becoming tomorrow's despair and hopelessness.

Finally, teach them the power of forgiveness. Since some forms of adversity can be self-inflicted or stem from mistreatment by others, we can either choose to let it consume us or let it go through grace and forgiveness. (Admittedly, this is easier said than done—but it can and should be done.) It's been said that bitterness is like swallowing poison and expecting the other person to die. Forgiveness is the antidote to that poison. When we forgive, we don't just release the other person, we release ourselves from being tied to the offense. This is an important, life-altering lesson for our young people—and all of us—to learn.

Here are some helpful questions as you help build a strong perseverance foundation in your young adult:

» Do they accept that adversity is part of life—that you love them unconditionally and don't expect perfection?
» Do they persevere through challenges by taking one step at a time and keeping up faith and hope?
» Do they accept that some adversity can be good for us and may make sense later on down the road?
» Do they embrace change and unexpected challenges as an opportunity for growth?
» Do they seek out their family and trusted friends for help when adversity strikes, rather than stuffing it in and hibernating?
» Are they able to forgive themselves and others when adversity is "for cause?"
» Are they willing to use the lessons from their adversity to inspire and encourage others?

It's important, as you work towards establishing these pillars in the lives of your teens, that they *know* how much you believe in them and that they, in turn, believe in themselves. The gifts of preparation, empowerment, and belief are priceless to our children. In fact, they're flat out necessities! These gifts will help set them up for success in life and give you the reassurance of a job well done. And, you'll help them build a leadership foundation that's as solid as a rock.

TRY THIS:

VALUE YOUR VALUES

Do your teens know their values—and how to hold on to them? It's important to identify what principles you are basing your life upon—and then stick to them at all times. One slip-up is all it takes to derail your plans!

Teens should recognize there are many decisions they can make right now that can have devastating effects their overall development and well-being, or that could deprive them of future opportunities, successes, and growth. This would include behaviors that could cause immediate physical injury (e.g., fighting or dangerous, thrill-seeking activities), with cumulative negative effects (e.g., drug use), or that could damage their reputation and close doors of opportunity.

Making the *wrong* decision in these risky situations can also result in their missing out on the normal activities and milestones of youth. Bad decisions in the values arena can preclude them from graduating from high school, attending college, realizing their career dreams and from enjoying close friendships and activities with their peers.

Using the list of values found on page 146 of this book, invite your teen to pick ten that he or she would identify as the most important and why. Each family member can pick his or her top ten in order of priority.

This is not an opportunity to lecture, but rather to explore ideas and opinions. All of the values are important, but some will be more important to some than to others. Use this as a chance to understand your teen's thought process. Share personal stories about times when your values were tested. What happened when you compromised? What happened when you stood firm and took the high road?

With a solid leadership foundation, your teen will be well-positioned to make key upcoming decisions right the first time.

TAKE FIVE

Here are a couple of scenarios you can discuss with your teen. Talk through what the decisional options would be in each case, which values would come into play, and what might be the outcomes of different decisions in each. Can you come up with other scenarios?

» You are invited to a party where you know there will be alcohol. You really like these people and want to fit in with them, but you're not sure this is the best way to do it—is it? Explain your rationale.

» It's time for finals and you've been working overtime at your job earning extra money to pay for a car that you want to buy before graduation. You know your college hopes are riding on your final GPA. You have a golden opportunity to get the answers to the final exam in your most difficult class. An "A" would guarantee you the GPA you need. Should you cheat, just this once? No one will ever know.

CHAPTER FOUR

PREPARE THEM FOR KEY LIFE DECISIONS

Life is the sum of all of your choices.
Albert Camus

A few months ago, I (Dennis) ran into a friend and successful business-man whose kids were about to enter an elite private high school. He had just ended a frustrating conversation with the principal regarding the lack of life skills training in their curriculum. For example, he was shocked to hear there were no personal finance courses. Clearly, a college prep school of this caliber would offer students a subject as essential as this, wouldn't you think? Apparently not. The principal's defense was that this was some-thing to be taught in the home. (Right!)

We may assume the schools cover these important decision topics, but the schools often think it's the parents' turf. So, based on misplaced assumptions or priorities, many key life trainings simply fall through the cracks. Unfortunately, it's the students themselves who bear the conse-quences, if we parents don't take the lead.

The same is true of topics like the college academic transition, career readiness/employability, independent living, and marriage and family. Some schools offer some of these courses, but mostly in the form of elec-tives. Even though they're universally relevant subjects, they're not required of all students. The end result is that life-preparedness is a hit and miss proposition at the school level. Regrettably, only roughly 10 percent of the educators we meet at conferences have defined for their programs the characteristics of a well-prepared graduate for life. If you don't define it, aren't you less likely to deliver it? Hmm!

At a time when our young adults are experiencing major life *changes*, they're also making critically important *decisions*. That's a lot of pressure at a time in life when they're not the most objective or wise. (I know I wasn't!) Because parents can't assume that schools or universities are helping that much, parents have got to take ownership.

With that in mind, let's turn to these key decisions our teens will be making as adults. Your children will be far better equipped to make these decisions right the first time, if they're made from a position of strength and with practical wisdom to guide them. The decision arenas are covered in detail in Chapters Seven through Ten of *What I Wish I Knew at 18*, but here is a summary of the key takeaways:

COLLEGE/UNIVERSITY ACADEMICS

I entered my freshman year of college with all the confidence in the world. (And, I'm not referring to the 2.5/1.0 female to male student ratio!) I was a solid 3.8 GPA in high school so what was there to fear?

And then reality punched me squarely in the gut. I knew something was fundamentally wrong after I received the lowest grade in my Cultural Anthropology exam. That's right . . . from 3.8 to rock bottom! It was a good thing my parents weren't paying for my schooling!

All told, this high school rock star concluded his freshman year of college with a 2.85 GPA. It was demoralizing and worrisome. Thankfully, I figured it out in my sophomore year.

There are several reasons the transition into college academics is more difficult than most imagine:

» The competition is stiffer
» The grades are fewer (so it's hard to recover from a disaster)
» Professors show less grace and rarely offer extra credit

» Mom and Dad aren't there to bug you with homework and alarm reminders

» Distractions are omnipresent!

» The pressure is greater because it costs money. Lots of money!

Not wanting to wish my freshman year academic story on anyone, I describe in *What I Wish I Knew at 18* my self-taught study method that immediately turned my grades around and eventually led me to become valedictorian in my MBA program at the University of Washington. Same brain, different study methods! The key secrets involve:

» Developing a study schedule that allows four days of review time; this relieves the pressure that comes from last minute cramming.

» Using the "Rainbow Highlighter Method" of progressively reading and coloring sections of the book/notes that need to be read and reviewed again. Each time, you use a different color highlighter in order to visually narrow down the sections that need to be further reviewed. This allows for multiple reps of the most difficult material and is a huge confidence booster, as more material is recalled at each iteration.

» Answering the easiest essay questions first (so you have more time to reflect on the harder ones while you're answering these) and using as many keywords as possible.

When it comes to college academics, it's a whole new ballgame. If that's where your teen is headed after the launch, be sure he or she understands this and develops his/her study habits accordingly. Help them avoid making the same mistakes I did! Have them talk with other students about the professors they're considering. And, don't place too much pressure on them to repeat their high school performance. It takes time to adjust and a little grace will mean the world.

CAREER

From the moment our friend Nancy entered Kindergarten, she wanted to be a teacher. Determined, she majored in Elementary Education and breezed through it . . . or at least most of it. In her final semester of her senior year, Nancy would take her practicum and couldn't wait to put her passion into practice.

But, there was just one problem. She *hated* it. Her dream career wasn't a match after all, and it was devastating (emotionally and financially). Nancy is now working on a Plan B, extending her college career and adding to her debt, because she didn't thoroughly research the fit.

This true story is incredibly common. Given the importance of career, one would think that colleges would bend over backwards to help students pick a well-matched major. However, this is often not the case. Many advisors are not familiar with "a day in the life" of particular careers, so their perspectives don't always translate to the real world. Also, the average student changes his/her major some three times. I was no different.

Adding insult to injury, it doesn't help that youth unemployment is so high, depriving teens of valuable, real-world experience. Many college grads are getting their first job after graduating. Is it any wonder why young people are indecisive when selecting a career?

Their career choice is one of the biggest decisions young adults will make after they leave the nest. Much of it will be influenced by their classroom experiences, which are outside of your purview. There are, however, some key fundamentals you can help develop in your teen beforehand—both in selecting and advancing in their career:

» **Career selection:** Encourage them to thoroughly research this decision, considering inputs, such as interest, skill, qualifications, personal fit, job outlook, stress level, and income requirements. It's essential that they speak with veterans in those fields who can give them the real-world scoop.

» **Building an edge:** Offer suggestions on how they can develop a winning competitive edge through experiences, education, and accomplishments; accomplishments that will help them stand out from the crowd. The competitive landscape is tough!

» **Marketing themselves:** Provide input on their strengths and how to persuasively convey them in an interview and in their resume; many young people are ill-prepared for interviews and how to present themselves as a compelling candidate.

» **Building their value and promotability:** Provide perspective on how to deliver on-the-job excellence and prepare for the next step. If they haven't had a job before, help them understand the qualities of a workplace MVP (as described in a later section).

Additionally, there are some key skills that will help them land—and succeed—in the job market. You can help them develop these areas to distinguish themselves in today's competitive marketplace:

APPRECIATE THE VALUE OF NETWORKING

You've heard it said many times: "It's not *what* you know, but *whom* you know." Of course, this is an overstatement, but in this high tech, interconnected age, it's truer than ever. The sooner your teen understands this reality the better.

No matter how talented we are, we all need people who will go to bat for us, both personally and professionally. Their invaluable assistance can take the form of introductions and connections, references and advocacy, decision-making in our favor, an information source, or general help. They help us gain access to strategically important people. They are one of our key personal asset categories—our network of contacts. Our ambassadors. Our very own sales force!

The employment recruitment process has changed night and day since I was younger. Nowadays, it's all about online applications that seem to disappear into the proverbial black hole—it's SO impersonal and frustrating. Somehow, some way, our application needs to stand out. No doubt about it, the best way is to have an insider advocating on our behalf. It adds a measure of dependability and reassurance to the hiring manager, and that's huge. It may not land us the job, but it helps get us into the game.

Our son Michael is a natural networker. Ever since he was young, Michael always enjoyed being with adults. He became a basketball ref at an early age and loved pick-up games with guys decades his senior on the golf course. Interestingly, connections from these circles were instrumental to his acceptance into the college of his dreams. And, today, they've proven just as helpful as he's entered the workforce. Thankfully, when it comes to networking, he values it and is good at it. And, dad loves to see him in action!

But, for many, networking doesn't come so naturally. Some are more reserved, some haven't developed the skills, and some don't appreciate just how important it is. So, parents, this is a great opportunity for you to influence and empower! Here are some key ways you can help:

> » Share the value of networking on both a personal and professional level.
> » Stress the importance of making a great first impression with *everyone* they meet.
> » Point out that future advocates are enlisted by demonstrating excellent character, cultivating the relationship, and showing appreciation. Help your teen understand that ambassadors put their reputations on the line when they advocate on his or her behalf! Motivate your teen to develop a reputation as a person of excellence.
> » Encourage them to get involved in various opportunities and spheres (i.e., "put yourself out there!") where they'll be able to interact with adults in different circles. *Networkers take the initiative!*

How do your teen's networking skills stack up? Who are their advocates? How can they expand the list? What are your opportunities to help them become a master networker?

BECOME A WORKPLACE MVP

There was a time when jobs for high school and college students were plentiful. Today? Not so much. Jobs for teens and young adults have become tougher to come by due to a sluggish economy and tighter employment regulations.

Regrettably, there is one other factor at work—employers are often preferring older applicants to younger ones. Why? Older candidates are generally considered more reliable with a stronger work ethic. Also, they show greater respect of authority and the senior position of the employer who is hiring them at their convenience. Young people who enter the workforce (or a job interview!) with any sense of entitlement will be in for a rude awakening. One young lady in the area just lost her job for calling in "sick" five minutes before her arrival time, going to a beach party, and proudly posting pictures on Facebook. We hear stories like this from employers of young people *all this time*. Don't let this be your child!

With all this in mind, how will your teen set himself or herself apart and flourish in a perfectly matched career? The answer is to first help him or her understand and embody the qualities of an *MVP* employee. Next, your teen will need coaching on how to deliver *excellence* in the eyes of an employer—that means demonstrating the qualities employers value, delivering excellent job *performance* and *contributing to their employer's success*.

DEMONSTRATE THE QUALITIES EMPLOYERS VALUE

Congratulations! Your son or daughter has just been promoted to store manager and earned a 20 percent pay raise! He or she is now responsible for the store's results, and his or her pay will be directly linked to its financial success. What qualities will your teen manager look for in the people he or she hires and promotes? A paycheck and a job are at stake!

Have your teens compare their list of desirable qualities with those most valued by today's employers:

Reliable	Globally Aware
Enthusiastic	Motivated
Trustworthy	Independent
Hard working	Dedicated and loyal
Innovative	Team player
Courteous	Excellent Communicator
Accurate	Leader
Adaptable	Well mannered
Positive	Good humored

These are worthy qualities indeed! So, here's your challenge: How would you and those who know your teen best rate him or her on these same qualities? And, how would your teen rate himself or herself on these attributes? What are his or her strongest areas and which need strengthening?

Bottom line: would you hire them? Now, be honest! And, would they hire themselves? If not, you've just begun charting a course for improvement.

In this highly mobile and professional economy, employers are also paying a premium for *teamwork skills*. Your future adult will be collaborating with different people on different projects throughout his or her career, demanding excellent interpersonal skills with people from all walks of life. It won't always be easy—some are easier to get along with than others, as we all know.

Here are the hallmarks of a great team player:

» Deliver excellent, reliable performance in their areas of responsibility
» Demonstrate a positive attitude that inspires and encourages his or her teammates
» Disagree in an agreeable manner and always listen actively and respectfully; focus on "what is right" rather than "who is right"
» Welcome constructive feedback

How does your teen measure up as a valuable team player?

DELIVER EXCELLENT JOB PERFORMANCE

Perhaps the most obvious hallmark of an MVP employee is excellent job performance. Translated, this means delivering top-quality results with a winning attitude and "can do" spirit. And, it means being easy to manage from the perspective of their supervisor who will evaluate their performance and determine their pay raise!

Here's a success tip that will help them immensely. Most supervisors will describe their job responsibilities and evaluation form to a new employee. Often, employees are rated on a scale, such as one to five on a number of factors (five being "excellent" and one being "well below expectations"). Interestingly, however, most supervisors will not *define* what constitutes "excellence." Therefore, if your teen's goal is an excellent rating (and he or she is not a mind reader!), here's what he/she should do:

1. Ask the supervisor what he/she considers "excellent" in the different rating categories (they'll be pleasantly surprised, if not shocked, by the question!)
2. Ask what would represent the most significant possible achievement he or she could make in the next performance review period
3. Deliver it with diligence and passion!

If the supervisor defines excellence and your son or daughter delivers the goods, he or she will be well-positioned for a great performance review. And, they'll also set themselves apart from the crowd!

CONTRIBUTING TO THEIR EMPLOYER'S SUCCESS

Many employees are highly regarded by their companies, but few earn MVP status. With hard work and the right attitude and methods, your son or daughter can be one! It involves going above and beyond the job requirements by contributing to the employer's overall success. Here are some real-life examples:

» Improving company sales and customer satisfaction through excellent service

» Offering innovative ideas

» Identifying ways to improve efficiency and quality and lower costs

» Leading important projects and initiatives

» Developing and leading others

» Solving challenging problems and being considered a "thought leader"

Being an MVP employee will serve your teens well throughout their careers. First, they'll develop a reputation for excellence, maximizing their career potential and promotability. Second, they'll strengthen their earning potential as many positions have performance-based pay. Third, they'll gain invaluable references for positions they may seek in the future. Fourth, they'll be less likely to be laid off in a workforce reduction (they're too valuable to lose!). Finally, and most importantly, they'll receive intrinsic personal rewards for a job well done.

It's theirs for the taking! Be sure your teen understands what it takes to be an MVP in the workplace, and that they have the character and "soft skills" to deliver excellence. For a host of reasons, far too many young people are coming off to employers as unreliable, unmotivated, undisciplined, and socially lacking. Yours needn't be one!

LOVE AND MARRIAGE

Unbeknownst to me, I selected a college known for its nursing and elementary education programs. Not that I knew that ahead of time, but I sure didn't complain! I met my college sweetheart there at a dance where we were matched by a computer. Whoever programmed the code was genius. (My guess is he or she now works for e-Harmony.)

Many young adults meet their eventual partner in the four years after leaving home. I came oh-so-close. Now, my perspective has totally changed as a father who is about to launch his daughter into college. Whoever the lucky guy is, he'll be tested worse than boot camp!

Seriously, it is a rather imposing thought that our children might meet Mr. or Mrs. Right outside of our direct supervision. It means we need to offer our best wisdom, so they make the right choices, especially with a relationship that's meant to last forever. Careers can change, but this one isn't supposed to! Are your teens prepared, just in case?

Some key themes to cover are:

» Taking a "3D" approach to dating, which includes being *discriminating*, *discerning*, and *deliberate*. Instead of BFF meaning "best friends forever," how about "best friends first" when it comes to a love relationship?

» Understanding the difference between "love" and "lust"

» Accepting that love takes time *and* timing! They say you meet four people in your life you could marry. Sometimes timing is the key ingredient to a successful relationship.

» Since it's meant to last forever, you have to think differently. It means *thoroughly* exploring compatibility on many dimensions and being as objective as possible. And, be prepared to accept the warts, because they probably won't change.

» Understanding the qualities of successful marriages and observing how the relationship measures up as it develops. Identifying the potential risks and asking themselves whether they can live with them.

With a 50 percent plus divorce rate these days, I don't think we can over-prepare our teens for this big step. Thinking about marriage well in advance and going into it as objectively and patiently as possible can make a big difference in the rest of a person's life. So will a healthy dose of self-respect and lots of wisdom, courtesy of their parents and other third party voices.

FINANCES

Remember that fun Sixties song, "Wonderful World?"[4] You know, the one that starts with "Don't know much about history, don't know much biology . . . ?" Here's my adaptation, and it goes like this:

Don't know much about budgeting;

Don't know much about investing;

Don't know much about a credit score;

Don't know much about free cash flow;

But, I do know trigonometry;

And, I also know geometry;

What a well-prepared grad I will be.

It's unfortunate, but so true! We are a financially and economically illiterate nation and it's showing—everywhere. Most of us parents weren't taught personal finance in school and only recently are we seeing more schools offer such courses. Ironically, most of the math we use in life involves managing our finances (unless we have a math-heavy career). It requires skill in adding, subtracting, multiplying, and dividing and, now and then, we use exponents and calculate present values! (I was a high finance investment manager and I never used calculus, trigonometry, or geometry.) I'm delighted to see more interest among schools, because our students need to understand how to *apply* math in life. Now, if we can convince colleges to require personal finance courses for admission, we'll really be talking!

I would guess that, other than "the talk," money is the least favorite topic parents discuss with their children. How can it be otherwise when most of us weren't taught it ourselves and when we're not necessarily the world's best role models? Regardless, it's a vitally important arena to cover, because we cannot count on it being taught in school or college.

There are many books, courses, and workshops on this topic, but we would recommend offering at least the following perspectives for financial foundation-building with your teens (Appendix B has a more complete listing of financial success principles):

» Since money is one of the three assets we have to offer (the others being our time and talent), it's an important responsibility to take seriously.

» Being a wise manager of money involves being financially literate, a diligent earner in your career, a disciplined saver and investor, a savvy consumer, a cautious debtor, and a cheerful giver. Good financial training should address these and other topics.

» They must learn how to live within their means, manage a budget, and generate positive cash flow (income minus expenses)

» It pays to give first, save and invest second, and live on the rest. Most people do it in reverse and live paycheck to paycheck. It doesn't work.

» Most financial problems stem from having high fixed expenses (including debt and credit card payments) relative to income; this often stems from having more house or car than they can realistically afford.

» They need to invest early, regularly, and as much as they can in a globally diversified investment program—preferably implemented automatically on a monthly basis

» They need to understand the difference between needs and wants and how to avoid impulse spending.

» When it comes to credit cards, train them not to spend more than they would if they had paid cash and to pay off the monthly balances in their entirety.

Additionally, they should understand the workings of the economy and financial markets through courses, media/networks and periodicals. They'll also need to know the basics of developing an excellent credit rating, banking and balancing accounts, insurance, loan applications, tax preparation, and avoiding identity theft.

To the extent you can, invite them into your world when it comes to money and finances. For example, use your shopping trips as educational experiences. Much can be learned when you explain the reasons for your purchase decisions and how much money you saved. Watch some financial shows together. Help them to understand what's going on in our economy and in the financial world. You'll learn something too!

Finally, you can teach your children great values through the use of money. That's right! Here are some examples:

» *Work ethic and commitment to excellence:* help them understand the link between pay/promotions and performance; praise hard work and point out excellence when you see it; at restaurants, invite their feedback on the service you received and how that should be reflected in their server's gratuity

» *Patience and self-discipline:* teach them the concept of "delayed gratification" by saving up for purchases (and restraining impulses) or investing for the long term.

» *Generosity and compassion:* seek out opportunities for your children to use their time, talent and money to help people less fortunate; give some of your (and their) money to charities they're passionate about and instill an attitude of gratitude by being thankful for the blessings you have. Mission-related trips/programs are particularly eye-opening and life-changing for young people.

SET THEM UP FOR THEIR "NEW FINANCIAL NORMAL"

Many from our generation personally experienced being starving college students or newlyweds on a shoestring budget. We knew that when we left home, it might be awhile before we worked ourselves into an income bracket that would secure the comfortable lifestyle we enjoyed growing up. We were willing to sacrifice and be content with less, because we accepted it as part of life.

Is your teen prepared to live on a much more conservative budget, when he or she leaves home and is living independently? It's an important question, because if they're used to big spending (and all the name brands) under your roof, it'll be hard to resist when they're in charge. They'll be more at risk of living beyond their means, or of making life-altering decisions based on a desire for quick money *now*.

In our home, we far "underspent" our income for this, and many other reasons. Jeanne and I don't want our children to be fixated on things (especially really expensive things!) and we don't want them to feel any pressure or entitlement to sustain an overly expensive lifestyle—especially when they're just getting started and their incomes are more modest.

Today, many young adults are struggling with this issue by overspending and running up high levels of debt in the process. You can do yours a lasting favor through good modeling while they're still at home and by previewing a new financial normal that's more realistic and conservative. Teach them how differently you'd live on the salary they're likely to make at the start. Help them develop budgeting and priority-setting skills. And, be sure they understand the risks of having too much house (or rent) and car.

Trust me—one day they'll thank you for it (even if they're not too thrilled about it now!).

Training your children about money needn't be overwhelming or intimidating. Focus first on getting the principles right and you'll be well on your way.

SOME FOUNDATION-BUILDING STRATEGIES

Some of you (especially single parents!) might be thinking, "This is all fine, but how on earth do we do all of it?!?" Rest assured, this is a journey where the sooner you start the easier it will be. Also, you might take an inventory of which areas could use the most strengthening and focus on those first. Here are some other helpful suggestions as you help build your child's leadership foundation and decision skills for life:

» *Model*-Whenever possible, demonstrate the qualities described in the personal leadership foundation. Children learn best from personal observation and they will notice whether you "walk the talk." Live it.

» *Involve*-Seek opportunities to involve them in your activities and decisions. Case studies with active participation can bring these skills and qualities to life.

» *Observe*-Look for opportunities to observe others, whether in the real world or on TV/movies. Call out when you see behaviors, attitudes, and decisions that reflect honorable leadership and when they don't. When they witness it in others, it forms memorable impressions.

» *Recognize*-Praise your son/daughter when he/she demonstrates the qualities and wisdom of admired leaders.

» *Train*-Some attributes and skills will require instruction; share your knowledge and wisdom as a coach and be sure to tell them your failures as well as your successes!

» *Role Play*-There are fun role-playing and game opportunities for some of the training areas (e.g., interviews). Keep it light . . . the "good stuff" will sink in.

» *Invite*-Encourage other trusted adults to lend their support and wisdom, as well. Affirmation from others is invaluable.

YOU CAN DO IT!

We all share different backgrounds, upbringings, and current family situations. Some of us came from loving and stable families with healthy modeling, while others didn't have those advantages. Growing numbers of children are being raised by single parents who face extra challenges in covering all the bases and nurturing confident and healthy future adults. Also, many parents lack the educational or professional background that their children will be pursuing.

Any of these situations can lead to feelings of insecurity and overwhelmedness. After all, we want the best for our children and the security of knowing we've prepared them well.

Because I was the first in my family to attend college, my parents could offer little in the way of college, career, or financial preparation. (Nowadays, there are organizations and programs such as AVID that offer resources and mentoring for first-time college attendees in their families.) I had to figure those out on my own. But, I did receive exceptional character modeling from them and their unbridled belief in me. That turned out to be more than sufficient for me.

Regardless of your background and current situation, you CAN cover the bases and help build a solid preparation foundation for your children. And, if your upbringing and family history has been difficult or worse, YOU have the opportunity to be the generational change agent! You can do it!

TAKE FIVE

Review the Parenting Preparation Checklist in Appendix D. Which areas are areas of personal strength for you? (Give yourself a high five!). Which areas could use some strengthening? Highlight these and rank them in priority order. Depending on how much time you have left before the launch, start taking steps to implement these items into your discussions and planning strategy with your teen.

Check back with the list in a few weeks, in a few months, etc. Are you making progress? It feels good to check things off a list, doesn't it? Done!

Part Two:

Relationship Preparation

VALUE YOUR TEEN'S UNIQUENESS

AFFIRM THEIR IMMEASURABLE WORTH

COMMUNICATE AND RELATE!

KNOW THEIR THIRD PARTY VOICES

"I don't even recognize this kid anymore! He seems to listen to everyone else but us. He doesn't tell us much at all and I'm feeling like we've lost control. *Have* we lost it?"

Sound familiar? One of the most challenging experiences for parents of teens is the transition in their communication and relationship. Sometimes it feels like we're being squeezed out. Our kids are changing so much. When this stage comes along, it puts new stresses on our relationship.

How can you confidently prepare for and navigate these times? The next four chapters offer tools to help understand your child's uniqueness and promote his or her self-discovery and sense of worth. We'll talk about some effective communication strategies and tactics that can build your "relationship capital" with your son or daughter. And, we'll discuss how you can develop positive third party voices in the life of your teen that will support your family's values and goals without you always having to be the one to reinforce them. (It really does take a village!)

Here's to healthy relationship-building and communication that will set you up for a lifetime!

CHAPTER FIVE

VALUE YOUR TEEN'S UNIQUENESS

*Today you are You, that is truer than true. There
is no one alive who is Youer than You.*
Dr. Suess

Do your kids know you value them for *themselves* and relate to them *personally*? Surely you've realized, especially if you are raising more than one child, that no two are alike—not even twins.

My (Arlyn) oldest and middle children, Tyler and Hayley, are practical, dependable, loyal, and task-oriented. They like order, stability, and predictability in their environments and relationships. My number two, Heather, is free-spirited, idealistic, and independent. She prefers limited structure, and appreciates opportunities for expression, creativity, and spontaneity. Tim, number four, is my most introspective child and the deepest thinker. He is logical, witty, and straight-shooting—you always know where you stand with him. Hillary, number five, not only likes to live by a schedule, but also likes to make the schedule AND be in charge of it!

By temperament, I'm more like Heather. My husband, Doug, is on the more laid-back and methodical end of the spectrum. We all complement each other in a number of ways. But, can you begin to imagine some of the sparks we've all had over the years, because of our different combinations of personalities? I shudder to think of the relational disasters we *could* have had, if we hadn't learned to understand each other.

That's why there's something very important we parents need to consider. Even the most well-intentioned preparation efforts in the world will fall on deaf ears unless we have a strong relationship with our teens that will allow most of our messages to get through. They need to know you care about them *personally* and *individually*. Don't think this is automatic. A good relationship between any two people, parent-child or otherwise, rests on the platform of mutual respect and valuing the other's unique gifts and contributions. Your child has characteristics that make him or her special and that set him/her up for a unique destiny. Just because we're shooting for the same *objectives* for our teens (e.g., solid leadership foundation, character, integrity, clear goals, sound work ethic, healthy boundaries), doesn't mean we can necessarily use the same *methodology* for each of them. Teens vary remarkably in their needs, reactions, communications, and behavioral styles. This impacts how they respond and relate to us and to the world around them.

At the same time, *parents* vary in these same respects, too! This is (one place) where parenting can get rather tricky—and, if you're not prepared to deal with it, very frustrating.

SO LIKE YOU (OR SO *NOT* LIKE YOU)

Sometimes people will say of a child, "Oh, he's just like his father (or mother)!" Other times, you wonder if you're even from the same gene pool or planet!

Parenting a child who is similar to you can be easier because you might naturally understand him or her better. It can also be harder, because you might rub each other the wrong way. This is particularly true when both parties have strong personalities and like to be in charge. Competition! Fireworks!

Parenting a child who is much different from you has its own set of pros and cons. When you have dissimilar personalities, you can complement one another. On the other hand, understanding each other can be difficult, because you approach things from such different perspectives.

The point is, we must be students of our children's temperaments and personalities—the way they are designed, so to speak—in order to work with that design and accomplish our objectives. Can you imagine how a house would turn out if the builder never consulted the architect's blueprint? Disaster! It's much the same with raising kids.

HOW PERSONALITY INFLUENCES YOUR PARENTING

Every child is unique and every parent is unique. It follows, then, that every parent-child relationship is distinctive, as well. There is no pairing exactly like yours with each individual child, even within your own family. Each family member has his or her own behavioral style, temperament, and even idiosyncrasies that have an effect on the others. Understanding this and using it to your *advantage* and not to your detriment, is especially key in the teen years.

Your teen's temperament and personality are what drive his motivations, behaviors, choices, and interests, and the way he connects with you and other people. At the same time, your temperament and personality do the same for you. Understanding how your teens are wired AND how their personalities interact with yours can help you:

1. identify what motivates (and discourages) them,
2. appreciate their strengths and be empathetic toward their challenges,
3. communicate in such a way that they receive your messages in the manner intended,
4. respond to them in such a way that they feel safe, heard, and understood,
5. refrain from overly imposing your own nature, preferences, and ambitions on them,

6. have realistic expectations of them,

7. respect your differences, and

8. develop parenting strategies that work best for all of you.

THE DISC PERSONALITY ASSESSMENT MODEL

Midway through our parenting career, Doug and I were introduced to a personality assessment model that greatly enhanced our ability to understand and communicate with our children (and each other, but that's a different story!). It's called the DISC® model. That's not to say there aren't other great assessment resources out there. But, this is the one that really helped us in our parenting.

The DISC Personality Profile is based on the work of renowned psychologist Dr. William Marston, a contemporary of Carl Jung. Marston developed the DISC Personality Profile in the 1920's, after studying the personality traits, behavioral patterns, and instinctual reactions of thousands of individuals. As a result of his work, Marston developed the DISC assessment as a tool for measuring four primary behavioral traits:

Dominance (D)
Influence (I)
Steadiness (S)
Conscientiousness (C)

Marston never actually developed a DISC assessment to measure these four styles. In 1940, however, Walter Clark took William Marston's work and developed the first DISC assessment—the same one still in use today.

Using the DISC model, we can group people according to their pace (fast or slow) and priority (tasks or people). There is no right or wrong (we all have a style!), and everyone falls somewhere on both of these continuums.

What might this look like? Let's pick a (theoretical) person and say his pace and priority of life could be plotted as follows:

X

1 (Slow)	**PACE**	(Fast) 10
Values stability and support		Values activity and change

X

1 (Task)	**PRIORITY**	(People) 10
Values task accomplishment		Values relationships

Now let's superimpose those lines onto one another in a perpendicular fashion to create four quadrants. The two points above, plotted on the graph below, would appear as follows:

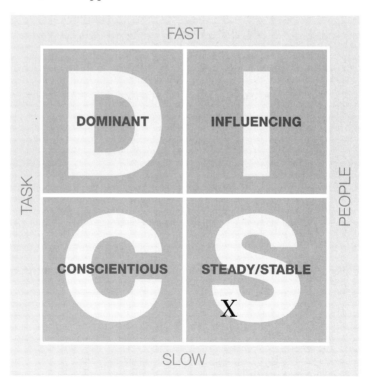

In the illustration above, our candidate, who is on the slower paced end of the spectrum and whose priority is people, would fall into the "S" or Steadiness quadrant.

Try it for yourself. Generally analyze if you prefer a faster or slower pace of life, based on the following criteria:

Fast pace: Outgoing, involved, a talker/teller, takes initiative, a risk-taker, active, makes decisions quickly, competitive, assertive

Slow pace: responsive, reflective, a listener, thoughtful decision-maker, quieter in groups

Now plot yourself on the spectrum above on a scale of 1-10. Do the same for your priority (your motivation). Do you place a higher emphasis on the completion of tasks, or on relating to and interacting with people?

Tasks: independent, thrives on accomplishment, fact-oriented, time-conscious, detailed/analytical, likes to be in control, guarded in relationships, principle-oriented

People: relational, interactive, interdependent, expressive, warm, supportive, not so concerned with time, flexible

Next, plot yourself on the priority spectrum on a scale of 1-10. Transfer these to the corresponding quadrant in the illustration above. In which quadrant did you land? And, are you positioned more toward the center of the diagram (in which case your behavioral tendencies are more muted) or toward the corners (where your tendency is stronger)?

D – Dominant – *Decisive, confident, self-directed, independent, direct, a change-agent*

I – Influencing – *Relational, interactive, expressive, visionary, emotional, fun-loving, optimistic*

S – Steady/Stable – *Dependable, loyal, committed, supportive, cooperative*

C – Conscientious– *Self-disciplined, cautious, detailed, analytical, intuitive*

Where you land in the spectrum will indicate what your personality, motivations, priorities, and comfortable pace look like in real life, as you relate to the world around you, including and especially your kids.

One mom told us, "My husband Bill and 17-year old son, Jason, butt heads constantly. There never seems to be a moment's peace in our house. Bill has high expectations of Jason and criticizes him constantly. But it seems like Jason deliberately does everything he can to antagonize his father and do the opposite of what his dad expects. Why can't he just listen to Bill's concerns and take them to heart? Why does Jason always have to push back, have another opinion, and be so antagonistic? I'm walking on eggshells, just waiting for the next argument to erupt . . ."

Sound familiar?

As we explored this family's personality styles using the DISC model, it turned out the dad, Bill, was a High C. Perfectionistic and detail-oriented, he had a strong sense of the "right" thing to do and wanted to make sure his son always knew what that was. His motto was, "Any job worth doing is worth doing *well*." If that meant taking a long time, if necessary, to do something with excellence and according to standard, so be it. As High C's generally are, he was a corrective parent—wanting to communicate high standards and enforce compliance.

Jason, on the other hand, was a High D. He was forward-thinking, independent, and liked to make decisions quickly and intuitively, without having to talk through the details and ramifications of each step. Jason wasn't as concerned with quality as his dad was. "Get in, get done, get out" (as quickly as possible) was his motto. As High D's generally do, he valued the destination more than the journey. His biggest complaint about his relationship with his dad was, "According to him, I can never do anything right, so why try?"

Was it possible for Bill and Jason to learn to get along, and create a relationship in which Bill could effectively communicate valuable wisdom to his son in this crucial season of life? Absolutely! It would start by Bill understanding what Jason needed in order to feel secure, validated, and empowered. When these intrinsic needs are met (in any of us), mutual trust and respect are established and real communication can take place.

Note the focus is not on changing the *other person's* behavior. It's been said that you can't change other people; the only person you can effectively change is *yourself*. And that's how Bill and Jason are going to learn to get along. That's how Bill is going to create a relational platform for preparing Jason for the real world, where not everyone will be like him, not everyone will respond to him the way he likes and not everyone will see things the way he does.

As parents, we hold the senior position in our relationships with our kids. That means we have to go first! Learning what our kids need from us—and adjusting our communication style and expectations accordingly—is key to cultivating the mutual trust and respect necessary to prepare them well for the road ahead.

RELATIONAL NEEDS OF THE FOUR DISC PROFILES

In the scenario above, it was eye opening for Bill to understand that his constant corrective input was rarely received as helpful, and, in fact, undermined his platform for communicating with Jason. Because Bill so valued doing things correctly, it never dawned on him that other people—especially his son—would not feel grateful to know "the right way to do things."

Because the details of any given situation were so important to Bill, he didn't understand why they weren't as important to Jason.

When Bill could appreciate that as long as the end result was good, and that how Jason got there was not as important, he was able to relax and loosen the reins. This meant taking a broader view of things and not requiring so much attention to detail from Jason.

Bill made a concerted effort to be more realistic and less perfectionistic in his expectations. He began giving Jason greater freedom to make decisions without having to talk through every nuance of the process. When an issue came up about which Bill had concerns, he started asking himself, "Is this a hill I want to die on?" (He was a former Marine.) Basically what that meant was, how strategic is this issue in the bigger picture of life? If it's not crucial to accomplishing the greater mission, Bill decided it's better to let it go.

Do you know what your teen's *relational needs* are? Here is a brief overview of the four styles:

HIGH D's VALUE:

» independence and autonomy
» winning, competition, and success
» taking action and achieving immediate results
» competency, action, personal freedom, challenges
» a frequently changing environment

HIGH I's VALUE:

» social recognition, group activities, and relationships
» friendship and happiness
» taking action, collaboration, and expressing enthusiasm
» attention, prestige, and/or popularity
» freedom of expression and democratic relationships

HIGH S's VALUE:

» cooperation and sincere appreciation
» opportunities to help
» stability and security; controlled environment
» loyalty and group acceptance
» personal accomplishments

HIGH C's VALUE:

» knowledge, expertise, accuracy, and quality work
» maintaining stability, space, and control over their environment
» diplomacy and tact
» careful analysis and attention to detail
» unique accomplishments
» personal growth

This simple overview of the DISC model is enough to help you do a quick assessment of most anyone and to quickly ascertain his or her intrinsic relational needs. Keep in mind everyone is a combination of the four styles, in varying degrees. Each person will have a primary and at least one secondary style.

I (Arlyn) am a high "I" with secondary "C" and "D" tendencies, depending on my environment. As a writer and editor, my "C" (Conscientious/Compliant) emerges. As a mom or a manager, the "D" (Dominant) kicks in! It's a good thing my High S husband brings the qualities he does to our marriage, parenting, and household. We complement each other well and are a great team.

PARENTING BY DESIGN

For us, understanding the need to parent, communicate with, and relate to our children individually and according to their own design was a breakthrough in our parenting. That's not to say we didn't have objective standards in our household. Obviously, there is a place for discipline and training in the child-rearing years that is appropriate and essential. Our values remain absolute. You don't lie, you don't cheat, you don't disobey, and you ALWAYS get home by curfew.

However, there are many things that should not be absolute. Say, for example, your teenage son wants to take up archery and automotive repair instead of the soccer and basketball in which you've encouraged him to excel. It turns out he's a High S/C and prefers activities that are more one-on-one, where he can experience personal accomplishment and have control over his own environment and performance. That may be hard for you to understand if you're a competitive, achievement-oriented High D or an extroverted, relational High I. But if you want a real relationship with your teen and a platform for mutual trust and respect, you'll need to manage your own expectations and learn to appreciate and respect his unique design and intrinsic needs.

Parents, we need to go first in these things. I cringe when I hear parents describing their relationship with their teens as if they are two junior high students bickering. We can't let ourselves be offended by the immaturity of our children. We have the benefit of years of life, experience, and wisdom. *We* must be the ones to take the high road.

As the adult in the relationship, we can take the lead in modeling what it looks like to take other people's personality and relational needs into account and adjust our own behavior and expectations accordingly. And, guess what! Not only will your own relationship benefit, but also, it will help your children relate with others they encounter in life.

MANAGING OUR OWN EXPECTATIONS

Speaking of expectations, perhaps you've heard of Tiger Moms. The term "Tiger Mom" originated with a sensationalistic book about the supposed superiority of Chinese parents who produce high achieving kids through a dictatorial parenting style. The author of the book said in an article she wrote for the *Wall Street Journal*[5]:

"A lot of people wonder how Chinese parents raise such stereotypically successful kids. They wonder what these parents do to produce so many math whizzes and music prodigies, what it's like inside the family, and whether they could do it, too. Well, I can tell them, because I've done it. Here are some things my daughters were never allowed to do:

» attend a sleepover
» have a play date
» be in a school play
» complain about not being in a school play
» watch TV or play computer games
» choose their own extracurricular activities
» get any grade less than an 'A'
» not be the No. 1 student in every subject except gym and drama
» play any instrument other than the piano or violin
» not play the piano or violin."

Wow! I wonder what her kids would have *liked* to do—and how this laundry list of rules and constraints will square with her kids' own definition of a fulfilling life.

Our expectations of our kids can have a huge impact on them, both good and bad. Good, in that we (hopefully) inspire them to excellence and give them a compelling vision for life. Bad, on the other hand, when our expectations violate their unique designs and create discouragement and resentment.

I recently spoke to a group of eighth-graders on the topic of relationships and communication. In the course of our classroom discussion, I conducted an informal survey of the students and had them evaluate where they landed on the "pace" spectrum. One thirteen-year old boy asked, "Do you mean what does our pace of life actually look like? Or what we *want* it to look like?"

When I asked him to explain, he went on to say, "Well, I have soccer three days a week, music lessons once a week (and I practice an hour a day), plus we have this and this and this . . . " I lost track of the other activities he mentioned, but what stood out most to me was his comment, "We've got something going every night of the week, but what I'd really like to do is *just stay home sometimes*."

I'm guessing this was a High S kid with High D or I parents. I'm also guessing there is the potential for some major conflict, or at least resentment, to arise in the next few years when he seeks more independence.

We *should* expect our children to do well—according to their aptitudes and capabilities. We *should* expect them to work hard—but also to have fun. We should expect them to be involved, according to their own interests and talents. But, we also need a sense of proportion. Are you seeing how parenting by design can affect our expectations?

A LITTLE BIT OF UNDERSTANDING CAN GO A LONG WAY

Expectations management starts with understanding our children's unique strengths and weaknesses. In nearly every situation I've encountered where parents and teens are experiencing conflict, this is at least one of the underlying problems, if not the main problem.

When we treat all of our children the same (or expect them to be like us) and fail to make adjustments to our expectations and parenting style based on their unique needs, we set ourselves up for an inevitable and epic fail. That's why it's important to know the areas of our children's unique designs that can create challenges for them, especially when they cause direct conflict with our own behavioral styles.

All strengths have corresponding weaknesses, and no one DISC quadrant is "the best." Some general *challenges* for the four DISC styles, when taken to the extreme, are:

High D's – impatience, stubbornness, need to "win," self-sufficiency, need to be in charge, impersonal

High I's – emotionalism, talking too much, impulsivity, disorganization, lack of self-discipline, egoism

High S's – aversion to change, lack of enthusiasm, lack of initiative, not speaking up for themselves, no sense of urgency

High C's – perfectionism, being overly detailed and nitpicky, being judgmental, worrying, sensitivity to criticism

AFFIRMING YOUR TEEN'S WORTH BY UNDERSTANDING HIS OR HER DESIGN

Your teen's sense of worth—"self-esteem," as is it popularly called—encompasses his or her beliefs about himself as well as his or her emotional response to those beliefs. We talk more about worth in next chapter, but we'll touch on it a bit here now, as it relates to a child's unique design.

Embedded in your teen's self-worth is the capacity to feel confident, be happy, and successfully address life's challenges—not to mention the everyday things like doing well in school, maintaining healthy friendships, and being a generally responsible and well-adjusted member of the family and community. Low self-worth can result in a number of psychological, physical, and social consequences that may influence how well our children navigate the teen years and the inevitable transition to adulthood.

Sadly, and all too often, these consequences can include depression, anxiety, suicide, eating disorders, gang involvement, angry outbursts and violent behavior, sexual activity, dropping out of school, and substance use.[6] Research also suggests that low self-worth during the teen years produces longer-term outcomes, such as fewer years of post-secondary education, greater likelihood of joblessness and financial difficulties, as well as poorer mental and physical health and higher rates of criminal behavior.[7]

This is why it is vitally important that our children understand and believe they are valuable, important, and loaded with unique potential—*and the first place they need to hear it is from us.*

"What!" you may be asking? "My kid is not getting his homework done, won't pick up his room, does nothing but play video games, and walks around with his face in his phone, texting all day. How do you expect me to praise *that*?"

We don't.

What we do want is to affirm our kids in *who they really are.* This demonstrates we know them, we hear them, and we believe in them—despite some of the immediate (and, admittedly, annoying) issues you may be experiencing.

Many times when parents see negative behavior emerging, the tendency is to tighten control. We try grounding. Loss of privileges. Restriction of freedom. Withholding money, car, and phone. No TV. Or, we increase our input level and turn up the volume. We resort to lecturing. Nagging. Yelling. Belittling. Criticism. Sarcasm. Frankly, it doesn't work, but our frustrations get the best of us and we persist. Unfortunately, some families resort to emotional or even physical abuse. This REALLY doesn't work.

What do all these accomplish, other than to drive our children further away from us? Some of these behaviors may be occasionally effective in the short-term. But in the long haul, they are usually ineffective and often destructive. They can lead to a loss of self-worth and an erosion of the parent-child relationship.

Instead, try becoming a student of your children and find ways to honor his/her unique strengths, based on his/her own unique design. Look over these lists and see if there are statements from the right-hand column you can substitute for any on the left that you might say to your teen.

INSTEAD OF...	TRY...
HIGH D	
You are so stubborn.	You are very determined.
Sit still for a change!	I realize you need to burn off stress by doing something physical.
You're cocky.	You're a confident person.
You're rude.	You have an honest and direct way of expressing how you really feel.
HIGH I	
Why can't you get organized?	You are relaxed about details and loose ends.
You are unrealistic.	You are optimistic and you have a great imagination.
Why do you always need to be the center of attention?	You are very likeable. People love to be around you!
You need to plan ahead more.	You are flexible and like surprises.
HIGH S	
You are stuck in a rut.	I know you're not crazy about change. I understand.
Why can't you go more quickly? Get moving!	You don't like to be rushed.
You're a pushover.	You are sensitive to the needs and feelings of others.
You're such a procrastinator.	You need to know what you're doing before you start.
HIGH C	
You're so picky, such a perfectionist.	You are committed to always doing your best work.
Stop pestering me with questions.	I understand you need details.
Get out and meet people!	You are a quiet person and content with just a few good friends.
Cheer up. Don't be such an Eeyore!	You're a serious person. You think deeply about things.

Do you see how perspective can make all the difference in the world to how we perceive and communicate with our kids?

Parental disapproval and communicating unmet expectations (whether verbally or non-verbally) can cause long-term hopelessness and damage to our kids' sense of self-worth, if we're not careful in our communications. What do your kids get from you when you correct or discipline them? Do they feel you try to understand their motivations, or do they simply feel judged and rejected?

When it comes time to offer input or correction, stop for a minute and check your own perspective. Are you seeing your teens through the lens of who they are, or whom you think they *should* be?

Note that we're not talking here about an "anything goes" mentality. We're not suggesting you let character issues slide in the name of personality differences. What we are promoting is the idea that a little understanding, perspective, and give-and-take can go a long way, when it comes to relationship and communication between parents and teens.

HOW YOUR BEHAVIORAL STYLE INFLUENCES YOUR PARENTING

Maybe you are connecting a few dots in your mind, as you quickly evaluate your family according to the DISC model. Perhaps you are already identifying the reasons for some of the challenges and frustrations you may be experiencing with your child.

All the unique strengths (and corresponding weaknesses) of behavioral styles are as applicable to parents as they are to teens. That means that where there are variances, there are going to be conflicts. These differences are not necessarily bad; they are just, well, different! It's also helpful to share your personality profile with your teen, Learning to see one another through this lens can be a breakthrough in your parent-child relationship. There is power in understanding. And, as your role and influence moves from driver's seat to passenger seat (and eventually to back seat), the relationship is very, very important. In fact, we would go so far to say it is foundational in terms of your ability to have credibility with your teen and a platform for communication and input.

If you are a High D parent, perhaps you are frustrated trying to get your High S teen moving and motivated. Your High I daughter is driving you crazy because she is so easily distracted and can't seem to stay on task. And, you are in constant conflict with your High D son who is always challenging your authority and bossing other family members.

Maybe you're a High I parent whose High D son is totally out of control and you feel like he's the one running the household. You want him to like you, so you tend toward permissiveness. You are frustrated that your High I daughter has no sense of responsibility—but it's because you've bailed her out of her problems far too many times.

Are you a High S parent with visions of weekends spent enjoying quiet family evenings playing games, but your High D and I kids are always one-foot-out-the-door? And you know you need to have a serious conversation about grades and college plans with your High S son, but neither of you wants to initiate the conversation—so it all gets left unsaid.

Perhaps you're a High C parent, and you're about to lose your mind over the disorganization that follows your High I kid around like Pig Pen in a Peanuts® cartoon. And, all the reasoning you've tried with your High D son to get him to prioritize time for college applications and visits has come to no avail—and the deadline is around the corner. Your inner pressure cooker is about to blow!

Do you see how your own intrinsic motivations can influence how you perceive and relate to your teen?

Here's a thought. Instead of persuading, coercing, yelling, grounding, criticizing, or controlling, try *adapting*. That's not to say that these (very real) issues shouldn't be addressed. But when we do so with understanding of our children's unique design, an appreciation of how their design influences their behavior, and a recognition of how our own behavioral style affects our perceptions and reactions to them, we can dramatically increase our ability to influence them.

It is beyond the scope of this book to offer a complete understanding of the DISC profiling system. Furthermore, the DISC model is only one of a number of helpful personality assessments. The point is that in this key transitional season leading up to "the launch," we need to be students of our kids in order to communicate effectively and steer them well, according to their individual wiring.

It's helpful to share this information with your teen. Teens are in an important time of self-discovery. They don't know that everyone is not wired like they are and they don't know exactly how their parents are wired, either. They may feel that different is "bad" when it comes to personality differences, relational needs, and behavioral styles. Help them identify their own strengths and weaknesses—and be honest about your own. This is a helpful item for their life skills tool box that will serve them well in their relationships with you and others.

TRY THIS:

DISCOVER YOUR FAMILY'S PERSONALITY PROFILE

There are many good free online personality assessments. One we recommend is www.123test.com, which has a good DISC inventory. It can be a fun family project to have each person complete the profile and see what his or her style is. Use this exercise as an opportunity to talk about your differences, your similarities, and how you can all understand, respect, and work together better.

TAKE FIVE

What would you identify as your (and your children's and spouse's) personality styles? What do you consider the major strengths of your style? How about weaknesses? What are the strengths and weaknesses of the particular styles of each of your children?

Next, consider how your relationships with your teens may be influenced by your respective personality styles—not right or wrong, just how you're wired. What are some ways you can adapt your communication with (and expectations of) your teens, based on their unique design?

CHAPTER SIX

AFFIRM YOUR TEEN'S IMMEASURABLE WORTH

If you want your children to improve, let them overhear the nice things you say about them to others.
Haim Ginott

On a recent visit to a prestigious private school, I (Dennis) spent a whole day as the leader of a small group of high school students. Going into it, I figured these "fast trackers" were on top of the world and brimming with self-confidence. Was I ever in for a rude awakening.

In a nutshell, they fell into two camps. The first, and most gut wrenching, were the children from families that either had disintegrated or, at a minimum, where there were no expressions of love or appreciation. In most of these cases, there were no fathers involved in their lives, or if present, the relationship was dysfunctional. Several tearfully went on to say they'd *never* heard their parents say they loved them. I'll never forget these conversations. I still grieve for those kids.

The second category was the students from families enjoying professional success. These students were destined for the fast track but, interestingly, were just as fragile as the other group. However, their tears were shed because their parents only seemingly valued their achievements and demanded virtual perfection. These kids never felt good enough at home and rarely received affirmation about *who* they were as a person. Even though they were strong students, they still lacked a true sense of their worth.

Many of today's schools are struggling to deal with the desperation felt by many teens in their student bodies. It doesn't matter if the kids are affluent or if they come from poverty or the middle class. We hear it all the time from high school and college counselors, teachers, and administrators. Students are dropping out of school at alarming rates, getting pregnant, joining gangs, abusing alcohol and drugs, breaking the law, and so on. They have to know these decisions will compromise their future, but *they do it anyway*. A counselor at a local crisis pregnancy center told us she regularly encounters 16-year old clients who cry when their pregnancy tests are negative. They want a baby—because they just want someone to *love* them.

At their core, these actions are manifestations of a lack of self worth, and the hopelessness this condition breeds. Tragically, many young people give up all hope to suicide. It's painful to see. But, here's what's interesting. We also hear many success stories of students who turned their lives around and beat the odds. The common denominators? These children received love, mentoring, appreciation, and attention from caring adults who affirmed their worth, believed in them, and set high expectations. These students recount how their outlook on life has completely changed and how they're now mentoring others who walked in similar shoes. Their spirits are renewed and their futures are bright. They discovered they have purpose. They have value. They have *worth*.

A little bit of worth can go a long way. Imagine what a *lot* can do!

EVERYONE MATTERS

Remember that old Dean Martin song that goes, "You're nobody till somebody loves you?" Our kids have reinvented the message in songs like Ingrid Michaleson's catchy, "Everybody, everybody wants to love; everybody, everybody wants to be loved . . ." It's a common theme, and not surprisingly.

We *all* need to know we matter. It's important at any age, but especially

so during the turbulent teen/young adult years. In this stage of life, acceptance and belonging are like mega forces.

A teen's search for significance can be like an extended visit to a smor-
gas~~~ ~~ ~~ sample this and that group or person to find out where they
⁓ is meant to be their friend. Sometimes the pull is so pow-
're willing to change who they are just to feel wanted and
⁓e that strong.

gathering of high school freshmen at an area school, the
the peer groups as the nerds, brains, jocks, stoners (which
⁓ods"), and a few other names I'll leave to your imagination.
⁓aven't changed much since I experienced this myself at that age.
⁓hen I was in high school, I floated between the jocks and the brains.
⁓entually learned to focus on the person rather than the group and
stopped trying so hard to be cool and accepted. It was so much easier and
it worked! My self-confidence grew as I began choosing friends based on
mutual interests and values, rather than on some artificial group dynamic.
That's a hallmark of maturity and confidence we hope our kids embrace as
soon as possible—the sooner before the launch, the better.

During this critical time, we need to be very strategic about increasing
our influence and decreasing their peers' influence when building a sense of
worth in our children. We need to be pouring affirmation and reassurance
into them. Sometimes we'll need a megaphone to drown out the unfriendly
voices in the crowd. These can be some of the most gut wrenching times for
parents, because their children's pain can become unbearable.

The teen/young adult years represent the greatest period of self-discovery in life, and parents have a great opportunity to assist in the process.
Our children's fundamental identity questions of: 1) Who am I? 2) What
do I have to offer? and 3) What are my opportunities? need to be carefully
considered and nurtured as they progress through this period.

Unfortunately, answering these three key questions can be challenging,
because they're subjective and our self-assessments aren't fully accurate. The
reasons for this are varied:

1. We look at ourselves through our own biased lenses.
2. We don't always have the benefit of others' perspectives and often "undervalue" special qualities that come naturally to us but not necessarily to others!
3. We lack a comprehensive framework to understand our value, since the inputs come from a variety of sources (family, friends, school, workplace, etc.).
4. Depending on our self-esteem and home lives, we may have a healthy and positive view of ourselves or a decidedly negative one.
5. The quality of parenting and modeling varies tremendously.
6. Schools differ markedly in their approaches to personal development and assessment.

These can be significant complications for young adults who are still in their early stages of discovery and who are also making key life decisions (e.g., career, college, family, and finances). Unfortunately, many are woefully unaware of their assets at this time and are destined to make suboptimal choices. Assessments they take at school often focus on their aptitudes and career interests—helpful, but narrow in scope, especially when it comes to intrinsic qualities.

Also, teens are still living as dependents under the control of their parent(s) or guardian(s). The strength of their familial support structure has a profound impact on their identity, confidence, and sense of opportunity. Parental factors such as their love and relationship status, depth of involvement in their children's lives, education and financial status, and maturity and modeling all influence a child's self-perception and sense of worth. *Bottom line: the quality of our parenting has a huge effect on our children's sense of worth—something over which they have no control!* We all need to take this fact to heart.

Who am I? What do I have to offer? What are my opportunities?

The answers to these fundamental life questions will literally frame your teen's future. Mere *guesses*, so common at this time, will only build a rudderless ship that meanders the waters of life. *Clarity*, on the other hand, will foster purpose, direction, confidence, and a legacy of impact, where his/her unique nature, passions, and talents can be put to great use in life.

What an honor and privilege it is for parents to help guide the process of self-discovery! And, what a huge responsibility it is! With that in mind, let's consider some innovative ways to promote our teen's self-discovery and understanding of their worth.

TAKING A HOLISTIC PERSPECTIVE

Everyone deserves an opportunity for a fulfilling life. But, achieving this requires that a person comprehensively understands himself (or herself) in terms of mind, heart, body, and spirit. This understanding, so critical in the launch years, should include a variety of inputs and perspectives.

Here are some benefits of providing our kids with a big picture appreciation of their intrinsic worth:

» It breeds hope, vision, and focus. Understanding our full complement of assets reveals a more complete picture of our worth.

» It fosters belief in ourselves and our future, essential components to our health and well-being.

» It promotes personal dignity, self-confidence, motivation, and discipline.

» It helps identify opportunities that play to our strengths—sources of joy, fulfillment, contribution, and legacy impact.

» It motivates us to make positive life choices and live strategically and purposefully.

» It helps us reach our full potential.

A BUSINESS APPROACH TO PERSONAL WORTH

Bear with me now for a little "business speak." It might sound strange, but people and businesses share some important similarities. Both:

» are created for purpose and impact,

» serve others,

» have "assets" (things of value we can offer), and

» have "liabilities" that hold us back (at a personal level, we'll call them "constraints").

You might even be familiar with a financial report called a "balance sheet," which details a company's assets, liabilities, and net *worth*. Analysts use this report to help derive a company's value. Can you see the parallels? As it turns out, we can borrow a page from the business world to help discover ourselves and our worth. And, the best part is you don't even need your CPA!

Let me now describe an innovative adaptation of the corporate balance sheet that reveals how assets and constraints (and our worth or value) can be applied at a personal level. You can use this imagery and thought process to help your teen discover and appreciate his or her own immeasurable worth. You can even use it yourself!

ASSETS

Let's start with our *assets*—the good stuff. They represent positive qualities or strengths you can offer to yourself and others in life. Their *value*, unlike dollars and cents for a business, will be a function of: 1) how *well* they are used (honorably and wisely) and 2) how *much* they are used. In other words, the impact of your assets will be determined by their quality and quantity of use. A motivated person actively uses his/her assets, while an unmotivated person does not. This is a key determinant of whether a person reaches his/her full potential. Assets that are not utilized only have *theoretical* value.

Now, let's describe the nine categories of assets. Yes, nine! Your teens (and you, too) have assets you might never have considered, but they exist and are ready for full deployment.

Physical: These assets involve your physicality and body and are often used in careers, volunteer opportunities (e.g., coaching), and recreation. They include strength, speed, endurance, coordination, agility, flexibility, dexterity, and gracefulness.

Mental/Intelligence: These assets involve your mind and are used throughout daily life in our careers, decisions, communications, and knowledge pursuits. They include: intelligence, aptitudes, analytical/technical thinking, creativity, conceptual perspective, reasoning, problem solving, attention, verbal acuity, and comprehension. They, also, include subject-specific proficiency (e.g., math, language).

Behavioral/Psychological/Personality/Emotional: This is the most diverse of the asset categories. It has the greatest influence on *how we deliver* our assets and relate to ourselves and to others. They include our: disposition, personality traits, social/relational behaviors, communication, discipline, attitude, self-confidence, motivation, decision style, judgment, and emotional intelligence. DISC assessments fall into this category.

Support System: This represents the people in our lives who care about us and have our best interests at heart (e.g., family, friends, mentors, affinity groups). We can rely on them for love, support, security, guidance, modeling, companionship, and encouragement.

Experiential: These represent the skills and personal enrichment we have gained by offering ourselves and our talents. They are of significant benefit to future employers and include: work, community service, life skills, leadership examples, global perspective, credentials, accomplishments, roles, and awards.

Network: This represents our personal and professional connections with people we can draw upon for assistance, advocates, or introductions. Our network of contacts is particularly helpful in our careers, but is broadly applicable as well.

Spiritual/Inspirational/Values: These represent the collective aspects of our spirit, including our intrinsic worth, moral compass, values, faith/spiritual life, and the sources of inspiration and encouragement we can offer others (often through overcoming adversity). Examples of values are found on page 146.

Interests: Through knowledge and personal experience, we're drawn toward certain subjects and activities that stimulate us intellectually, physically, spiritually, or emotionally. They are used in arenas such as activities, intellectual pursuits, reading, hobbies, and recreation/leisure/entertainment/travel. Think of them as the "spice of life!"

Passions and Dreams: Our passions and dreams provide vision, direction, motivation, and a sense of purpose in our lives. They offer potential fulfillment and are usually based on our skills, interests, desires, or causes we care about. They are manifested in several life arenas including career, service, and family and significantly shape our destiny.

Clearly, you and your children have many unique qualities to offer—more than you ever realized.

CONSTRAINTS

Unfortunately, each of us also carries burdens and baggage that hold us back, distorting our view of ourselves and our strengths. They can damage our self-confidence and sense of worth and can breed hopelessness. They impair our performance and cause us to underutilize our assets. They can be overwhelming and lead us to behaviors and decisions that are contrary to our well-being and can compromise our future.

Some common personal constraints include a fear of failure, guilt or shame, abuse and neglect, inability to forgive ourselves or others, difficult family circumstances/poor parental guidance and modeling, a lack of support structure, and low self-confidence. We may have many assets to offer, but if our constraints are severe, they can impede our ability to see them or use them.

Addressing our constraints through self-reflection, mentoring, counseling, and prayer can have an even bigger impact than growing the value of our assets. By reducing the influence of our baggage, our assets become more freely utilized. For some, *yesterday's constraints* can become *today's inspirational assets*, when tough life challenges are shared with others through mentoring opportunities. Now that's transformational!

TRY THIS:

DEVELOP A PERSONAL BALANCE SHEET

Now that you understand the basic concept of a personal balance sheet, let's put it into action. What follows is an assignment that may prove to be one of the most valuable exercises you will ever do with your teens. At this seminal time of life, you can help them holistically understand themselves and their worth in a new way. Plus, it's inspirational and fun!

Help your teenagers develop their "personal balance sheet"— a holistic understanding of who they are and what they have to offer. The inputs should come from three sources:
1. themselves
2. other people (especially you!)
3. independent assessments where available (e.g., DISC, aptitude tests)

By having inputs from multiple sources, they will have a much more comprehensive and accurate appraisal of themselves. Here's how it works:

First, help them think of trustworthy people who know them well and have their best interests at heart. These may include family members, best friends, teachers, coaches, mentors, youth leaders, and the like. Priority should be given to adults who can offer perspectives with maturity and wisdom.

Second, have your son or daughter ask these trusted advisors to describe your teen's special qualities and strengths in each of the nine asset categories. (Note: most will have greater perspective in certain areas than others, so they won't answer for all segments.) Have your teen hand out the asset category descriptions with appropriate space to record the answers. They can also conduct these via personal interviews if more convenient. That way there are opportunities for discussion and clarification.

Also, have these advisors share anything they think may be constraining your teen or holding him/her back. (Note: Your child needs to be open to receiving the constructive feedback rather than defensive—this is for his or her personal benefit!) This feedback can correspond to the asset categories or not.

Note, before this outside input is received, encourage your teen/young adult to develop his or her own list of assets and constraints. This way, he can see how differently (and narrowly) he appraised himself versus the way others see him—both affirming his views and revealing new assets and insights. This will offer tremendous encouragement, inspiration, and perspective to your teen.

Third, have him or her incorporate system-based assessments where available. For example, there are free online resources for aptitude and personality tests.

Finally, for each asset category (and one overall constraint category), create a consolidated list that combines all of the inputs.

This is your Personal Balance Sheet. An abbreviated example is shown in Appendix D.

At the teen/young adult stage of life, when self-esteem is fragile and volatile, a personal balance sheet can prove as a formidable anchor and source of encouragement. Keep a copy of your child's personal balance sheet handy to remind you of your child's immeasurable worth in those times where you might not see it so clearly in his or her behavior. Use it to point out those aspects of their personality, character, gifts, and talents that make them unique and special, outside of their accomplishments and performance. It's especially helpful during those periods when their self-esteem is ebbing.

Having an understanding of one's worth and significance is one of the greatest gifts a person can receive. And, you can be the one to give it to them!

TAKE FIVE

Facilitating and encouraging our children's self-discovery is one of our greatest parenting responsibilities. Here are some helpful questions for building a solid foundation of self worth in your teen:

1. How well do your teens know who they are, what they have to offer, and what their opportunities are in life? How do you help facilitate their self-discovery and understanding?

2. How well does your teen understand his/her special assets in the nine categories? How would his or her list compare with the one you developed?

3. Have you and other trusted adults communicated your view of your teen's unique qualities and worth? What new assets were revealed?

4. When you honor your teen, do you distribute your praise across all the asset categories or focus on a few? How might you communicate more broadly to cover all the bases?

CHAPTER SEVEN

COMMUNICATE AND RELATE!

Don't worry that children never listen to you;
worry that they are always watching you.
Robert Fulghum

It was the summer of 2004, and I (Dennis) couldn't wait for school to start. Michael was about to enter his freshman year of high school, and I was about to become "Superdad." I would drop him off on my morning commute to work and we would have the time of our lives along the way. It'd be one deep father/son conversation after another and we would bond like Fixodent. None of this "absentee father" stuff for me!

So, imagine my excitement on "opening day," as we would begin a new chapter in our relationship. Not surprisingly, he seemed a little quiet that morning (it was a new school in a different city), which I attributed to "pregame jitters." No big deal, I'll just ask a few open-ended questions to jumpstart things. But, each was met with an indecipherable groan, as he searched for his favorite song on six different stations. Hmm. Twenty-five minutes later, we would reach our destination with nothing to show for our time together. After my well-wishing prayer, he was on his way. Hmm.

Clearly, things didn't go as planned, but it was no big deal, since we'd get the lowdown at dinnertime. However, our "How was your day?" was met with "Fine." And, our "How do you like your new teachers?" was met with, "Fine." Our unusually loquacious son was now a young man of few words. *That* was a switch!

In the ensuing weeks, I noticed this was becoming a pattern. My questions merely bred disinterest and brief responses. This Superdad was becoming Superdud! Was I losing my touch? Or, did I ever have it in the first place?

Then, one day it finally occurred to me. When I was that age, I never wanted to talk in the morning either! Maybe there was hope after all! But, my role had reversed—I was the dad now. I would need to develop some new communication weapons for my arsenal. Something told me this wouldn't be as easy as I thought.

After all, my bud had just become the big high schooler—and all that comes with that.

WHAT'S GOING ON?

I don't think we're ever fully prepared for this major parenting transition—especially as "first timers." Our children are facing many new experiences, changes, and challenges, as they enter young adulthood, but I never realized how much this would affect our communication and relationships. Some of their major developmental adjustments include:

» *Physical/psychological:* their bodies are undergoing major changes and growth that affect appearance, behavior, and emotions.

» *Mental:* their brains are rapidly evolving, which has ramifications on decision-making, concentration, and learning ability.

» *Social:* their identity and reputation are being formed, friendships are created and lost, and peer pressure/influence soars. Eventually, they endure the greatest social adjustment of all—leaving home and the security of their convenient support structure.

» *Responsibility:* they face additional responsibilities and duties commensurate with their maturation (e.g., employment, driving).

» *Decisions:* they face a growing number of life-changing choices involving college, career, etc. Each carries with it new pressures and uncertainties as they transition toward independence.

» *Familial independence:* as they advance through the teen years, young adults increasingly exert their independence and "test the waters." This is a natural progression to adulthood, as they transition from the "passenger's seat" to the "driver's seat" (and hopefully their parents are moving to the passenger's seat).

With all of this change occurring in a compressed timeframe, it's no wonder our teens and young adults become increasingly unpredictable and our tensions rise. It's the classic example of *push-pull.* Just when we want to draw them closer during this time of heightened pressure, they tend to push us away to exert their independence. Our offers of help aren't always appreciated or wanted.

This can be a tough pill to swallow for moms and dads—especially when children dismiss (or at a minimum, devalue) their advice, while embracing that *same* advice from others! (That's why I love to offer advice when their friends are visiting. There's nothing like having our kids' friends say how smart we are in front of them!)

It's important to understand that this is part of the natural progression to independence, rather than a sign that we're losing it. So, hang in there! It just comes with the territory.

LOOKING THROUGH THE PRISM OF OUR OWN UPBRINGING

Isn't it ironic that our greatest responsibility in life comes without an instruction manual? So much of our parenting can seem like trial by fire, learning as we go. We're guided by some vague recollection of how we ourselves were parented—for better or worse. Those memories are our "normal" and often frame our own parenting methods—again, for better or worse.

I was raised by loving, married parents who devoted their lives to their children. As is often the case, one parent was outgoing and highly communicative (Mom) while the other (Dad) was more reserved and focused on providing for us. I have very fond memories of my childhood, my upbringing, and my family. I *always* felt secure, knowing that my parents loved me and believed in me.

So, to the extent I've passed on any parenting methods from my mom and dad, that's been a good thing. The prism of my upbringing is a legacy gift from my parents for which I'll always be grateful.

Not everyone has enjoyed such an upbringing. Through no fault of their own, many are raised in dysfunctional homes by parents or guardians who didn't provide a safe, secure, and loving environment. As a result, their prism is distorted and discolored, absent of the benefits of a healthy parenting vision. Consequently, some perpetuate the same methods of their parents, repeating the vicious cycle. Others, through courage, counseling, and mentorship, find a way to break this pattern and make a fresh, healthy start. They are to be admired for overcoming enormous obstacles.

I share this perspective because, if yours was a difficult upbringing, the remainder of this chapter may seem like an idealistic dream world by comparison. That would be understandable. Even if what we're about to describe seems only aspirational at this point, it's a good place to start. Be encouraged that a new and better vision is possible and that we are *all* imperfect parents simply trying to do our best.

RELATIONSHIP BUILDING

It goes without saying that parenting is more art than science. After all, each of us, parent and child, is a unique creation with traits, interests, experiences, and dreams of our own. Before I became a father, I figured that parenting would be more standardized than it really is. Actually, it needs to be more customized than I ever imagined.

Jeanne and I started out with the rather naïve assumption that our kids would be just like us. That theory went out the window as our Michael began "revealing himself" as a youngster. We had given birth to a highly energetic and creative kid with an extremely high people orientation. He was pure "I" all the way (in DISC terminology), unique among our gene pools.

Meanwhile, daughter Lauren is the consummate nurturer with a steady nature. She is athletic and has a tremendous amount of self-discipline and maturity for her age. In DISC space, she has lots of S and D—polar opposites on the grid. Neither has career aspirations like his/her parents, which is fine by us. Clearly, there are no "chips off the ol' block" in our family! It's been a lot of fun, but with lots of surprises and things to figure out along the way.

All this to say, parenting isn't a cookie cutter proposition if we want to build strong and enduring relationships with our children. It takes a healthy dose of discernment, patience, trial and error, adaptability, and humility, if we want to succeed. Further complicating matters is that everything is magnified in the teen and young adult years, when there is so much change and pressure. It puts that much more stress on our relationships.

Setting our children up for a successful launch requires building a relationship that will endure through adulthood. We're still their parents, but we gradually let them go, increasingly treating them as adults. If we keep too tight a grip (like trying to maneuver a kite, but keeping it on a short string), they will be more apt to rebel after leaving home and your relationship will suffer. The image of releasing an eagle to soar, rather than a kite to be controlled is the perfect analogy. *You are increasingly assuming the role of coach, called to influence not direct.* It's a necessary transition we must make, for their good and ours (more about that in upcoming chapters).

With that in mind, we need to build lots of relationship capital with our children. Think of it as a measure of the overall health, well-being, and trust in your relationship. The necessary ingredients to maximizing relationship capital with our children are:

- » Love
- » Trust
- » Understanding

» Mutual respect

» Encouragement and belief

» Ability to forgive and seek forgiveness

» Appreciation for each other's uniqueness and value

» Engagement and commitment

» Shared interests and values

» Ability to communicate deeply and lightly

» Meaningful experiences and conversations

» Enjoying fun times together

Imagine a large bucket with a label: "My Relationship Capital with _____." Like the universe, this bucket has an unlimited ability to expand. Flowing into the bucket is a stream containing the above essential relationship nutrients. The stronger and richer the flow, the greater the willingness of your teen to share with you and involve you in his or her world. That's because the bucket level is an indicator of the degree of emotional safety, security, and trust your son or daughter feels with you.

However, because we're imperfect, so are our buckets. Leaks will inevitably spring, due to our decisions, attitudes, behaviors, and communications in daily life that compromise these ingredients. Often, these leaks come from "tests," when our teens exert their independence contrary to our rules.

Although our goal is an ever-expanding bucket, in reality the "water level" rises and falls. Our tendency is to focus on increasing the flow, when sometimes we really need to plug the leaks. That often takes the form of uncomfortable conversations to seek mutual understanding and correction (regardless of who is at fault). No one thrives on confrontation, but conflict avoidance will only exacerbate the problem in the long run. In these instances, *"Sharing truth in love"* is the operative message. Oh, how I wish I heeded this all the time!

A few more points about the relationship bucket are noteworthy. First, the level of capital will determine how deeply they will share and allow you into their world. Second, it influences how quickly conflicts can be resolved and forgotten. If capital is low, teens will shut down or rebel, compromising your ability to influence. If it's high, the conversations are less temperamental and resolution is easier to achieve. Third, because our children are dealing with parents individually, mother and father will have their own relationship buckets. While we strive to parent as a team, we still have our unique relationships. Sometimes kids are naturally more comfortable discussing certain subjects with one parent over the other and that's perfectly okay.

Take a few moments to consider your relationships with your children on the above dimensions. Which are flowing strongly and which could stand some improvement or additional investment? Are there leaks that could use repairing? What conversations are needed to achieve mutual understanding and growth?

As we discussed in Chapter Five, each person (parent and child) is uniquely designed with different traits and interests. Consequently, compatibility and relationship capital among family members will vary. It's important for each parent to understand his/her behavioral style to maximize relational effectiveness with each child.

A final thought on relationship-building with teens is the need to have the right "specs" in our communication. Especially during this time of life, the timing, subject matter, setting, and tone can make all the difference in the world. If even one is off, it can compromise your purposes. This requires extra parental wisdom and discernment, and it's not easy. Be on the alert for what works and what doesn't for each child, because they'll differ!

MOTIVATORS

According to the researchers at Performance Advantage, there are three top-ranked motivators of a workforce that can apply to a family. Simply stated, they bring out the best in people. They are, in order:

1. being *appreciated* and recognized for their value and contribution,
2. being included on decisions and *listened* to, and
3. having an *understanding* supervisor.

You're probably wondering what this has to do with parenting. The answer is, "A lot!" While most people would think the greatest workplace motivator is money, the reality is that all three of the top ones involve relationships and communication. And, they're all free!

These are especially effective when raising teenagers to be responsible and thriving adults. When translated to parenting, the above can be reworded to:

1. being appreciated and valued for their uniqueness, contributions, and growth,
2. showing them increasing respect and responsibility by involving them in decisions and listening to their point of view (i.e., shifting from directing to influencing), and
3. seeking to understand them.

Each of these helps develop greater independence, discipline, and responsibility in our teens. And, putting them to use helps address one of today's biggest issues with many teens and young adults—a lack of motivation. They also help us *value their person more than their performance*—vitally important in our parenting.

SPREADING THE LOVE

In addition to personality differences, our interests vary as well. Each family member has his/her favorite sources of enjoyment: recreation, entertainment, intellectual pursuits, hobbies, service, associations, and the like. How compatible the interests of each parent are with each child can have a significant impact on their relationship. If dad loves mountain biking and daughter loves ballet or if mom loves camping and son loves a posh hotel on 5th Avenue you can see how it can influence their relationship and how they spend time together.

In our family, Michael's and Lauren's interests are as different as day and night. He is non-stop and loves activity and entertainment. She values quiet time and reading. Through some creative adaptation, we sometimes take separate "guy vacations" and "girl vacations" with each inviting his or her best friend. It works!

When our interests are more aligned with one child, it's doubly important to spend as much time with the others. Children will naturally seek evidence of preferential treatment, even when none is intended. The greater the compatibility, the more likely the parent can, unwittingly, spend extra time with that child. We need to be balanced in our engagement with them. They'll notice if it's otherwise. So . . . enter their world and experience their interests, even when they're not your cup of tea. And when you do, don't nag them about how your preferences are better.

COMMUNICATION STRATEGIES THAT EMPOWER AND INFLUENCE

In order to set our teens up for success in adulthood and build enduring relationships, we must be effective communicators. We may have all the wisdom in the world to offer, but if we package it in an unappealing way, it won't stick. This section contains some practical strategies that will help fill your relationship bucket and prevent those damaging leaks.

Strategy 1: Meet them where they are.
It took me far too long to realize that Michael and Lauren were much more communicative at different times and places than others. Deep dinner conversations, chats during commutes, and all the times that were convenient for me often didn't work for them. I learned that our best conversations were away from home at coffee shops or restaurants. A change of environment made all the difference in the world in terms of their willingness to share with me.

Jeanne and I also learned that doing something with your kids (e.g., cooking a meal, watching a show, playing games, listening to music, taking a walk, building something, having a manicure or pedicure, or playing a sport) works. It seems a little distraction can take the "heaviness" out of a parent/teen conversation. It helps build relationship capital by enjoying the experience and the conversation.

Find the time and place that works best for your teen and *sacrifice your convenience for them at this critical time.* Notice which environments bring out more conversation and which don't and operate accordingly. If they're not in the mood to talk, let it be and don't take it personally (even when two minutes later they're chirping like birds with their friends!). Forcing it doesn't work. Believe me, I've tried!

Strategy 2: Focus more on understanding and listening.
Because parents have the benefit of experience and wisdom, it's easy for us to overly direct and control our conversations (especially for those of us "high D's"). The busier we are, the more we run this risk. We can easily do most of the talking and give them advice without listening to their perspectives and feelings first. Sometimes they just need to vent and only want us to listen. We can fall into a trap of prejudging and jumping to conclusions without giving them the benefit of the doubt and respecting their opinions. Without realizing it, we're devaluing them, harming our opportunity to influence and their opportunity to grow.

It's amazing to see the difference in our conversations, if our goal is merely to understand, share, and relate. By asking open-ended questions, valuing their opinions (even if you disagree), and focusing more on listening than talking, you'll build capital and grow deeper in your relationship. And, by all means, listen without any hint of condescension. That's a leak that will become a gaping hole in your relationship bucket!

Bottom line: think "share with" rather than "lecture to." They'll appreciate you for it.

Strategy 3: Value and recognize the person more than the performance.
We all want our children to do their best. But, isn't it more important for them to be their best? Over the past decade or two, our culture has been

breeding "performance parents." You know, folks who define their own identity and success by the performance of their children. You see it in the stands at Little League games and the desire for "bragging rights" when socializing with other parents. You, also, see it in parents who threaten professors and employers, when their children aren't given the best ratings, and in the chronic over-commitment of children to sports and other activities that run them into the ground.

I witness this firsthand when I speak with teenagers at schools. Many are heartbroken and resentful, because of the pressure they feel, the comparison to siblings who are performing better, and the comparative lack of interest by their parents in the *person* they're becoming. Increasingly, parents are living vicariously through their children and often depriving children of their own dreams. It's not healthy and it doesn't set them up for success. It only breeds resentment and insecurity.

Whenever possible, honor the admirable character qualities and behaviors of your children. Instead of simply praising their 3.5 GPA, honor their perseverance, discipline, efforts to improve, character, resilience, and dedication to excellence. Recognize their journey and what got them there, not just the destination. Express your pride in them, even when they don't take first place. Show them your love and belief is unconditional. Your bucket will overflow!

Strategy 4: Test the waters and start with positivity.
It's not uncommon for teens to experience greater mood swings for reasons we don't always know or understand. It's hard when the child who once shared the moon is now the aloof and uncommunicative teen. Sometimes they just need to be alone. We need to respect that. It's one of my biggest growth areas because I'm an analytic and so interested in their world.

When your teen is quieter than usual, it pays to test the waters with simple, non-controversial questions to take his or her "communication temperature." If his answers are brief, or his mood seems closed, give him space and let him know that you'll be around to chat if he wants. And, always try to start your conversations with a positive tone or topic. Even when we have tough conversation topics to discuss, it helps to get off on the right foot by saying something that will be appreciated. Negativity from the outset will only close the door.

Strategy 5: Invite them into your decisions and respect their opinions.
One of the greatest honors in life is to be asked for our opinion. In fact, as mentioned earlier, it's one of the top three motivators. So, knowing this, is it any surprise that one of the greatest honors to a child is to be asked for his or her help or opinion? It really stands out to someone who is usually in the subordinate position.

I'll never forget my vacillation and indecision when choosing a title for my first book. I developed a new list every day for weeks, but nothing stuck. Then, in a moment of exasperation, I decided to call Michael, who was a sophomore in college at the time. I shared my frustration and with not a second of thought, he blurted out, "Dad, why don't you just call it what it is . . . it's what I wish I knew at 18." I knew this was the perfect title from the moment I heard it. I should have asked him from the beginning.

Because we parents are older and wiser than our children, it's easy for us to fall into the trap of deciding everything ourselves. Yet, often our children can offer invaluable perspectives just like Michael did. If we are training future adults, it's imperative that we seek their opinions and help whenever we can. It's an honor for them to be asked and included and it can legitimately help with our decisions and understanding. We may not always agree with their recommendations, but that's okay. They are generally glad to be asked and that's what counts.

Strategy 6: Remember, how you say it can matter more than what you say.
It's easy to think that our words are all that matters, but nothing can be further from the truth. Our non-verbal cues and tone of voice can have far greater impact on how our communications are received than the content

of our message. And, when we work with young people who are transitioning into adulthood, it matters that much more.

Our attitude and tone are particularly important to get right in our communications with teens. If we come across as condescending, negative, angry, or irritable, they'll tune out or worse. Repetitive comments, excessive reminders, and above all, nagging, are to be avoided like the plague. It's best to defer our conversation to a better time if we're in that kind of mood.

Strategy 7: Fully engage and have fun!

One of the greatest relationship destroyers affecting families is busyness and over-commitment. During a recent speaking engagement, a father in the audience asked whether the key to raising kids is quantity or quality time. To his chagrin, my answer was, "Both." There's no way of getting around it.

Our time and how we allocate it to our children is profoundly important. It's one of the few things we can't do over and, to a child, it's one of the key indicators of our priorities. So, it's critical that we get this right and create the capacity in our busy lives to invest in them.

Also, commit to fully engaging in the lives of each child regardless of your tastes—even if it means attending concerts with musicians you can't stomach! Spread your love. Spread it well.

Finally, don't forget to have fun. During the teen/young adult years, there are so many key decisions that can be all consuming. Find time to chill, laugh, and enjoy good times just for the fun of it. It helps relieve the pressure and will encourage them to want to spend time with you—both now and in the future.

Strategy 8: Share in humility.

In life and in relationships, some things are "need to haves" and others are "nice to haves." At the top of the need to have list is *trust*. In the teen years, when children are exerting independence and facing new temptations (many of which are unhealthy), trust can quickly evaporate. It also is compromised when parents are unable to communicate difficult things in a loving way and to respectfully seek mutual understanding. When children don't perceive their parents as a safe outlet, no one wins.

One of the most effective ways to build trust is for parents to share their stories and past mistakes in humility. When a parent demonstrates vulnerability by revealing some of his or her "lessons learned the hard way," it demonstrates trust and respect to our kids. It conveys that we're not perfect (and don't expect them to be), and encourages them to share, too. At this age, the fear of failure can run deep, and it's reassuring for them to hear our stories, mistakes, and failures wrapped in humility. It's a powerful way to influence.

Strategy 9: Customize and analyze.

After devoting an entire chapter to the uniqueness of our children, it stands to reason that we need to customize our communications as well. They have different personality styles, biorhythms, and natural habits that we should take into account. That means "packaging" our content in different ways, not unlike how a sales presentation needs to be tailored to each unique audience.

Recalling the DISC behavioral designations, here are a few helpful reminders for communicating with our children:

	THIS WORKS	THIS DOESN'T
HIGH D	Directness/empowerment	Vagueness/emotional
HIGH I	Personal/conceptual	Detailed interrogation
HIGH S	Supportive/non-threatening	Dominance/pressure
HIGH C	Specific/examples	Vagueness/arrogance

This takes discernment, some trial and error, and analysis. When you have particularly great conversations, consider what made them so (timing, setting, topic, tone, and tactics). Then, when things don't go so well, do the same thing. The objective is to identify what works best and what doesn't with each child. By studying their engagement and demeanor you'll gain valuable insights. This will help set up your future conversations for success.

Strategy 10: Master these expressions.

Let's face it. Some of us express our emotions more easily and naturally than others. To generalize, it's easier for women to share their feelings than men. We're also influenced by our parents' approach. My family was classic—mom the expressive one and dad not so much.

In one of the success pointers in *What I Wish I Knew at 18* ("Express Yourself!"), I share some key phrases that are important for us to master. Take a look at the following list and ask yourself which ones roll naturally off the tongue and which ones don't. Each of them is important to communicate with our teens:

I love you	I'm sorry
I'm proud of you	I was wrong
I appreciate you	Please forgive me
I admire you	Thank you
I care about you	Let's agree to disagree

Notice how each of these expressions is empowering and builds trust and relational capital? If some don't come as easily to express verbally, remember that notes, cards, and letters are powerful tools in your arsenal, as well.

Strategy 11: Project their difficult situations onto a third party.

With new pressures and new experiences, the teen years offer special challenges and difficult conversations. Our children face tough situations (often socially), and we should hope to be welcomed into the equation to offer wisdom and advice.

A particularly effective strategy during tough times is to "project" their situation onto a third party in order to depersonalize it. You might recount a similar situation and how that turned out. Or, you might ask them how they would advise a friend going through the same circumstances or decision. It's amazing how this promotes a safe, sharing environment, objective decision-making, and empowerment. By doing this, they're more likely to apply this clear thinking to their own situation.

Strategy 12: Solicit and embrace their feedback.

No matter how hard we try, we'll always be imperfect parents. To complicate matters, we're in the lead position in the relationship and supposed to do the right thing! Often times, we don't.

One idea worth considering, especially if you sense some growing distance, is to ask your teens for some constructive feedback on your parenting. Frame your goal as developing a stronger relationship and see if they have any general or specific suggestions for improvement. Be sure they feel safe in answering and that you don't react defensively. You might be able to correct some misunderstandings and gain from their perspectives.

By asking for their feedback in humility, you might find some new currents flowing into your relational bucket and plug some of those nasty leaks you might not have realized had sprung up!

Finally, if you're a person of faith, this is a great opportunity to ask them to pray for you, your relationship with them, and the decisions you're making. You will honor them by asking and be blessed by their prayers!

WHEN RELATIONAL CAPITAL
IS DRY AND SPARKS FLY

Every relationship goes through its ups and downs. The volatile teen years offer an additional supply of opportunities for conflict and stress. They're processing a lot, and we as parents are trying to transition from control to influence. Often, a certain coolness permeates the air.

If your relationship capital has dried up, one strategy, recommended by consultant and Organizational Psychologist Richard Himmer, is FLPP. This acronym stands for conversations that are:

» Frequent

» Low Risk (avoid controversial topics that may trigger fireworks)

» Personal (meaningful to the individual—not just "how's the weather?")

» Positive (offer opportunities to affirm or praise)

These conversations can get things back on track.

Additionally, the relationship capital ingredients mentioned earlier offer ample opportunities to rebuild the trust and safety needed at these crucial times. Look out for fresh streams to add to your bucket and keep your eye on any areas that are springing leaks. When in doubt, share your thoughts and ask for their input.

Here are some key things for all of us to remember during times of disagreement and correction:

» Share your views in love rather than harshly or condescendingly.
» Keep your cool and resist the urge to fight anger with anger.
» Respect their point of view, even when you disagree.
» Avoid nagging, irritating, and frustrating them.
» End with a touch, hug, and expression of love.

Life can be hard, no matter how old you are, and frequently awkward to talk about. But, these strategies can help take some of the sting out of your difficult conversations.

LETTING GO WITH OUR WORDS

As we seek to empower rather than control our children, certain words should govern our behavior and occupy our communication filter: influence, ask, listen, invite, respect, understand, encourage, share, and inspire. These are especially helpful to keep in mind when tensions rise and when our children are making difficult decisions.

During our recent college search with daughter Lauren, Jeanne and I were struck by the comments we received from other parents, mostly moms. Lauren had narrowed her final choices to a university across the state and another far away. We were completely ambivalent, knowing both were outstanding choices. After all, we're releasing an eagle destined to soar.

With few exceptions, these other parents assumed that we would (or should) want her to attend the closer university. To a person, they were surprised to hear that location didn't even enter our minds. Rather, our focus was to help her choose the place that would best fulfill her dreams.

I hear and read many comments from parents (again, mostly moms) who really struggle with letting go. They celebrate their children's choices to stay nearer to home as though this was their goal all along. It makes me wonder how many messages, direct or subliminal, were made to their teens about how hard it will be to have them leave home. How are teens supposed to make a decision that's best for them when their parents' insecurities are echoing in their head? If our goal is to empower and release with confidence, our communications need to be aligned with that. Our kids are smart enough to pick up on any inconsistencies.

REMEMBERING OUR RELATIONAL GOALS

As our children transition toward adulthood, changing our filter from instructing to empowering should happen incrementally. We increasingly assume the role of influencer and encourager, rather than director, so our relationship and communication must change. This paradigm shift comes more easily to some than to others. Because our children and our roles are undergoing such significant transitions, it's important to keep in mind our key relational goals:

» We're raising future adults, not forever-dependent children.
» We must respect their desire for increasing independence and empower them to assume greater responsibility.
» We must strive to build an enduring relationship based on mutual trust, respect, and understanding. We must be viewed as a safe place for them to share their dreams, hurts, challenges, and disagreements.
» We must promote self-discovery and responsible decision-making, even if it comes with risk. Mistakes are a necessary part of the growth process.
» We must regularly model unconditional love, even when we don't always agree.

» We, as parents, must communicate as "one voice" so our children don't receive conflicting messages or modeling.

» We must demonstrate full engagement in their lives, no matter how dissimilar are our interests and how busy we are.

» We must be approachable and available—it takes both quantity and quality time!

» *Above all else, we must share truth and wisdom in love.*

While these communication goals are important for parenting children of any age, they're absolutely essential when raising teens and young adults. As you review what we've discussed in this chapter, consider whether your communication methods influence and empower, or direct and constrain. Remember, we're releasing eagles to soar, not kites to control!

TAKE FIVE

Take some moments now to reflect on the strength of your relationship with your teen and the quality of your communication. How has your communication style changed through the years? How does your style differ with each child? As you reflect, consider the following questions and be brutally honest in your answers. They will provide an excellent springboard for taking your communication, and your relationship, to new heights.

1. How has your own upbringing shaped your parenting methods and communication style?

2. How have you adapted your communications to your teen's growing need for independence and responsibility? As your teen gets closer to the launch date, is your communication becoming more empowering, or are you holding on for dear life? (Remember: wings, not strings!)

3. How would you assess the quality of your relationship capital with each of your children? Which components are strongly in place and which could stand some improvement?

4. Review the suggestions in the section, "Communication Strategies that Empower and Influence." Which work well for you? What other methods do you use that empower your children?

5. How would your teen view you in terms of approachability and availability? What changes can you adopt in order to improve this from his/her perspective?

CHAPTER EIGHT

KNOW THEIR THIRD PARTY VOICES

No one can whistle a symphony.
It takes a whole orchestra to play it.
H. E. Luccock

Has this happened to you? You tell your teenager something a hundred times over and get nowhere. Then someone slightly cooler comes along, says the same thing, and gets an instant response. You think, whaaaaatt?!

Don't worry. You didn't do anything wrong. It's a normal phenomenon!

Somewhere in the late middle school or junior high years, you probably started noticing something. All of a sudden your "little buddy" didn't want to be so buddy-buddy with Mom or Dad anymore. If your opinion *was* valued, well—now it doesn't seem to be worth as much. Increasingly, as the teen years progress, most moms and dads notice their teens pulling away and gravitating more to peers and other voices.

For many parents, this can be a source of angst and concern. But, it's helpful to keep in mind that this is a normal part of the maturation process during this season of parenting. Healthy people grow into their own identities and eventually get launched into the world to establish lives and households of their own. Failure to do so is "failure to launch" (reminiscent of a famous movie by that name). That's what we're trying to *avoid!*

Teenagers can be like rubber bands. Sometimes they stretch far away from us—as far as they can get—and then suddenly bounce back close. When it happens, don't take it personally. That being said, it pays to approach this phenomenon strategically, so the "rubber band" stretches and increases its reach, but doesn't snap.

During this time, it pays to get to know the other voices in your teen's life, both the good and potentially not-so-good. It will prepare you to understand, support, and let go at the right times with confidence (and to reel them in a bit when necessary). Some "voices" you'll want to be paying attention to are:

Other adults

Friends

Media/internet

Your home

Their inner voice (conscience)

OTHER ADULTS

Doug and I (Arlyn) have been fortunate to have many other sound voices in our kids' lives. They've been especially valuable during the teen years, when our children didn't want to hear so much from Mom and Dad. These voices have included:

» their grandparents and other extended family members,

» long-time family friends,

» friends from our faith community; youth group leaders/mentors,

» teachers and coaches who took a special interest in our kids and invested in them, and

» parents of some of their friends.

It's been rewarding to see the different perspectives and qualities these other "voices" have contributed to our children, especially at times when we were a little less popular. They offered wisdom in diverse areas like:

» work ethic

» integrity

» perseverance and self-discipline
» relationships
» financial management
» spiritual life (faith, encouragement, prayer)
» practical skills like construction, painting, cooking, and car repair
» the value of family
» aspirations for college and a successful career
» modeling a lifelong marriage

In a day and age when there are so many potentially harmful voices coming at our kids, it's essential to recruit a team of positive voices who can offer wisdom and reinforce the values we're trying to instill in them. Sometimes Doug and I intentionally went looking for such voices. Other times, they just showed up providentially.

One of our children had a quick temper that generally erupted when he failed to live up to his own extremely high standards. He found it difficult to accept anything less than a stellar performance from himself. Where this generally manifested itself was in sports. We tried to help him control the temper (and lower his expectations a bit), but were not having as much success as we wanted.

After a race one day, Tim lost his temper with himself one time too many and his track coach suspended him from the team. Instead of benching him completely, however, Mr. Eager made Tim his right-hand man for a period of time. Tim was expected to suit up for practice, help set up and take down the hurdles, and generally serve as the coaches' "gopher."

It was a great move, and one Doug and I applauded. Note that we didn't push back or question the coach's wisdom. We didn't enable our son by pitching a parental hissy-fit and insisting our kid get a fair chance to participate.

I am often disappointed by the behavior I see in some parents when their children are benched, disciplined, or simply don't get the playing time they think their kid deserves. What is that teaching them, other than (potentially) modeling entitlement? Doug and I have always made the effort to set an example to our kids by granting coaches and teachers the authority to do their jobs. Only once have we ever had to intervene when we felt a teacher was not acting in our child's best interest—and even then we did it respectfully through a higher authority and not in the presence of the child in question.

But, let's get back to our track scenario and how it paid off. The extra time spent with his coaches, not just then but subsequently, helped build a self-discipline and confidence into Tim that resulted in the success for which we were hoping. He turned into a fine track athlete (eventually qualifying for the state championships!) and a much more self-controlled young man through the help of third parties. Such is the power and influence of a coach's voice, among others.

Now, Doug and I had certainly been working on this issue with our son at home—but, at least this time, it was another voice that initiated the breakthrough. Is that because the coach had more wisdom than we did? Not necessarily. The unique value of other adults in our teens' lives is not just the wisdom they offer, but the fact that they are *listened to*. So, if our voices are temporarily devalued, we can recruit others to "shore us up."

Plus, sometimes other adults have unique perspectives and insights that we as parents simply lack. Besides being Tim's track coach, Mr. Eager was also his AP Psychology teacher. He was able to offer Tim unique insights that spoke directly and objectively to Tim's logical nature, helping Tim to better understand himself and his reactions. It ended up being a win on a number of levels.

This is one reason Doug and I joke all the time that parenting is a "team sport"—and our team extends beyond ourselves as Mom and Dad. Some experts believe the magic number is five—that every teen needs at least five adult voices in his or her life that will reinforce positive values and a healthy self-image. Do you have the benefit of other influences in your teen's life that will tell him the same things you would? Are there environments with which you could help connect your teen, in order for him or her to interact with helpful adults and mentors? Think about a service organization, faith community, team, or club. Look for ways to maintain regular times of interaction with family friends, grandparents, cousins, aunts and uncles.

If your teen is going through a rough patch, who in your life could become a great asset for this situation? It always pays to keep them in your hip pocket just in case.

FRIENDS
THE IMPORTANT VOICES OF GOOD FRIENDS

Make new friends, but keep the old; one is silver and the other gold.
~Girl Scout song, Sue Lynch

The increasing influence of peer friendships is an inevitable component of adolescence and another powerful voice in our kids' lives. Helping them navigate this aspect of teen life is more than "important." Later on in life, as they move into new environments such as college and the work force, the ability to develop trusted, positive friendships will be *crucial* to their success.

During the teen years, your son or daughter has likely developed friendships that are deeper, more exclusive, and more constant than in earlier years. These relationships provide teens with safety zones where they can feel accepted, explore who they are, and experience a sense of belonging. Here, they can practice the social skills they will need to navigate the real world for the rest of their lives. For all these reasons, peer relationships are a good—and necessary—part of our children's personal development.

Parents may complain, "My kids don't listen to me anymore," or, "Their friends matter more than we do." On the surface, this can appear to be true, especially when our kids seem preoccupied with their friends' opinions and sometimes inordinately influenced by their values. We worry they will succumb to negative peer pressure and submit to invitations to engage in high-risk behavior.

But, before panicking about your kids' succumbing to negative peer influence, stop and consider another perspective. Often, your child's friends, *if they are the right ones*, can offer some valuable motivation and feedback:[8]

> » to perform better academically,
> » to participate in sports, clubs, and other school activities,
> » to serve in community and volunteer efforts,
> » to develop qualities like loyalty, commitment, and teamwork,
> » to place a high value on family ties, and
> » to steer clear of high risk behaviors and stick to their values.

Here are some things you should know about teens and their friends:

> » **Teenagers often move in and amongst multiple groups of friends at the same time.** When they were younger, your children likely had a few close friends. Teenagers, on the other hand, are now exposed to more relational spheres (such as multiple classes at school, sports and clubs, community, youth groups, a job, etc.). Because of this, they will develop different circles of friendships with common interests.

> » **Teens will start to entertain friendships at multiple levels (as adults do).** Within their growing number of spheres, teens will develop close friends *and* casual acquaintances. Time spent with each may ebb and flow. They may become closer friends or pull back and move on. They might have close relationships with one or a few individuals. They might also belong to one or more "cliques" or groups of friends that are dissimilar to one another, but with whom they have a degree of affinity or similarity.

> » **Teens will try friendships "on for size."** I have remarked that my daughters seemed to change friends more often than they changed

clothes! As it turned out, these times were just a phase. While teens can have friendships that are constant and ongoing, they often move from one group to another. As class schedules, activities, and other involvements change, they might develop new friendships and lose others. Or, as mentioned earlier, they may discover that a friendship they were "trying on for size" wasn't such a good fit after all, and head for the exit.

All these aspects of teen friendships are preparing your son or daughter for the launch. What better time to find out where and how to make good friends—and when and how to tactfully withdraw from the not-so-good ones—while they are still in the security of home and their secure support system?

LEARNING TO MAKE (AND KEEP) THE RIGHT FRIENDS

We all know how intimidating it can be to be a new face in a new environment. Most people avoid those situations like the plague! Teens are especially notorious for being insecure about moving out of their established peer groups and into new ones. That's why the freshman year of high school can be so tumultuous—the same with college.

However, as we all know, making new friends is a reality of life and a challenge our young adults will face over and over. It might be when they go off to college or the military. It might be when they start a new job, move into a new apartment or neighborhood, visit a new worship center for the first time, or sign up for a fitness club. It's different for everyone, but one goal will be the same—assessing who has the potential to play a part in your life.

That's why it's important to teach teens how to cultivate new friendships with like-minded individuals who share their interests and values. We want them to understand the pitfalls of getting sucked into destructive relationships with negative people because they were desperate for companionship or to "fit in."

What are the principles we want to instill in our teens with regard to developing healthy friendships? Well for one, they need to know themselves and what's important to them, and look for friends that share those interests and values. You can teach them to:

» be self-aware of their personality style, interests, beliefs, and passions,
» know what hobbies, subjects, and pursuits they enjoy, and how they like to spend their free time,
» recognize the character traits and values they hold most dear and will guard at all costs, and
» identify particular causes or organizations they're passionate about and through which they can get involved and meet other like-minded individuals.

Once they develop answers to these questions, encourage them to look for opportunities to pursue those interests. Whether or not the people they meet *actually share* their interests and values can only be determined by trial and error—but at least they can learn to start putting themselves in the right spot to find them!

When it comes to friendships, I encourage my kids to cast a broad net (be inclusive) and then go slowly, ask questions, and spend exploratory time with people. As those individuals' interests and values are revealed, my kids quickly find out whether they are a potential long-term friend. Encourage them to gracefully bow out of a poor fit. When it comes to friendships, quality beats quantity!

Also, if patterns and behaviors indicate a poor match and especially if they possess destructive attitudes or actions—steer clear! Following are some clues.

WHEN PEER VOICES ARE NEGATIVE

The key is to keep company only with people who uplift you,
whose presence calls forth your best.
~Epictetus

While many friendships are positive and motivating, others can lead teens in the wrong direction. Here's when it's important to maintain a healthy relationship ("voice") in your teen's life in order to have the platform to step in with some well-timed words of wisdom.

Sometimes some friendships need to be cooled for the better interests of your child. You will usually observe the destructive effect of a negative peer influence by changes in your teen's attitude, respect, honor, energy, language, or disconnecting from home and family.

Creating distance between your teen and a bad friendship requires a delicate and strategic approach. While increasing *control* may seem a natural reaction, it can actually be more productive in the long run to increase *communication*. If you can ask the right questions, it's possible to help your teen discover for himself or herself that maybe this friend isn't such a great "friend" after all.

Here are some warning signs you can teach them to look for in their "friends":

» They ridicule your positive choices, values, and interests.
» They are highly critical, negative, and disrespectful—seeing the worst in people.
» They put pressure on you to enter their world despite your refusals. They use the "everyone does it" argument.
» They exhibit anti-social tendencies.
» They are involved with pornography, cults, or heavy substance abuse.
» They "bring you down," just making you generally feel melancholy, discouraged, and/or depressed.

Warn your teens that, if they find themselves in a relationship with someone like this, they should take steps to distance themselves. One of the most valuable lessons we can reinforce to our children is that everyone isn't meant to be their friend. This is an especially hard concept for your High I and High S children to grasp—they are relational animals, after all! However they need to understand it's not their responsibility to help and fix other people. There's a psychology term for toxic relationships like that and it's called *co-dependency*. It's beyond the scope of this book to address the ramifications of those kinds of relationships, but suffice it to say, your kids don't want to be in one!

Consider some pro-active strategies for helping your kids look for (and find!) positive friendships:

1. **Help them develop a healthy self-concept.** Teens who have a strong sense of self-worth are infinitely better equipped to recognize detrimental influences from their friends and to stand up for their values and beliefs. Does your child know his or her value? Do you communicate this in words, actions, and through appropriate trust granted?

2. **Train them how to cultivate good relationships.** The stages of relationship development go like this:
   » Acquaintance
   » Prospect (a *potential* friend)
   » Friend
   » V.I.P. (Very Important Person)

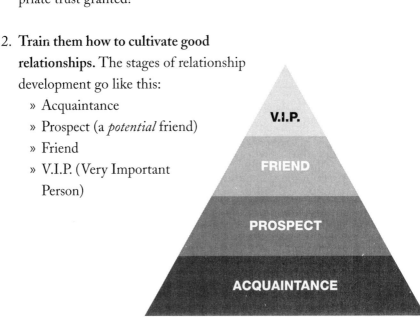

Every person who becomes more than an acquaintance will start in the first stage. Most stay there forever, while others may progress into the next stages. Only a very few will make it to the VIP stage—and that's the way it should be. Help your teens understand that true friendship is a process that takes time, trust, and timing!

3. **Teach them to recognize inner motivations.** Why would they want to get involved with activities that violate their values? Most teens don't like the initial experiences of high-risk behaviors. What they are attracted to are things like acceptance ("I want to *belong*."), image ("I want to be *cool*."), or adventure ("I want to be *free/invincible/powerful*, etc."). Does your teen know how to self-reflect and ask himself / herself the hard questions? Have you modeled this for him or her?

4. **Role-play getting out of bad situations.** Practice makes perfect! Maybe they won't ever encounter them, but equip your kids just in case. What will they say? How will they react? What is their exit strategy? It may seem silly, but practicing will serve your teens well, if they ever get in that situation. They won't just be hearing their friends' voices encouraging a mis-step; they'll be hearing *your* voice in their ear with some practical strategies for extricating themselves!

   In our family, we always had a secret word or phrase our kids knew to use when they were going to a party, or somewhere things could potentially get out of hand or awkward. We told them they should never be afraid to call or text us, no questions asked. We picked an innocuous phrase they could say to us on the phone in the presence of others, like, "I forgot to feed the dog." That signaled to us that something was amiss, without others knowing they were calling for their parent's rescue! Having that option in their back pocket reinforced the point that there was always an out and a safety valve.

Soon your teens will be out of high school, away from their secure relationships and off on their own. They will need to forge new friendships. Do they know how to recognize the right potential friends, and steer clear of destructive ones? Now is the time to practice.

MEDIA/INTERNET VOICES
WHAT IS THE ENTERTAINMENT CULTURE
SAYING TO YOUR TEEN?

There is a host of voices competing for our teens' attention and allegiance—not all of them human. The media, music and entertainment industries, and the internet are great examples. What are these all saying to your teen? And just how powerful a voice are they in shaping their values and behaviors?

The answer is, extremely. The typical American teenager:[9]
» watches approximately three hours of television a day,
» views TV an average of 17 hours per week and listens to several hours of music per day,
» spends more than 38 hours per week using media in general (TV, videos, computers, tablets, smartphones, and video games),
» uses the internet an average of two hours for four days per week, and
» has watched 15,000 hours of TV by the time he/she graduates from high school, compared to 12,000 hours spent in the classroom. No kidding!

Our kids belong to the most connected generation ever, technologically speaking. What used to be specifically TV watching has in recent years evolved into more varied device-watching. Today's teenagers are watching more video on mobile devices (computers, laptops, tablets, smartphones, etc.) and less on the traditional TV. Online, they shop, post and view photos, read messages and articles, chat, play games, and glean all kinds of information about the world and life in general. They walk around with headphones attached to their ears, constantly streaming into their ears playlists they've custom-loaded onto their iPods.

All this viewing, listening, and online interaction dramatically affects our kids. Every day they are receiving hundreds of messages about what is true (or not), what is important (or not) and what is cool (or not). The values they absorb from these voices can have a huge impact on their later success in life. Take sexuality, just for example.

Typical teen media fare consists of heavy doses of sexual content (at least inferred, if not outright depicted). Sex is often presented as a casual activity without risk or consequences. Don't think this doesn't affect our kids' values and choices! It has *tremendous* potential to distort their sense of reality. If kids see a behavior on TV and in movies often enough (or hear about it in song lyrics), they can start to think it's not a "big deal," even if personal or family values urge otherwise. Peers can reinforce this.

Recently, I was shocked when I finally listened to the words to a hit song I had been hearing on the radio. Even I had been toe-tapping to the beat! In it, the female artist was chastising her boyfriend for wanting too much from her ("too much" being a real relationship). What she wanted was only a "hook up." (And if you don't know what *that* means, you are really behind the times! It means "friends with benefits" with more emphasis on the "benefits" than the friendship.)

Really? Seriously? Tragically, yes.

So, guess what listening to these particular "voices" produces: earlier and earlier sexual activity.[10] Teens who said they listened to music containing overt sexual messages were found twice as likely to become sexually active within the following two years, as were teens who listened to little or no sexually explicit music. The same kinds of statistics are true of movies.

Regardless of what parents tell them is right, safe, or wise, media content is often a loud voice encouraging teens to act contrary to their (and their family's) established values. Does this mean we shut it all off and take away the tablets, computers, TV, and iPods? No. It *does* mean we should make an effort to know these voices in our child's life, just like we want to know what the other voices in their lives are saying to them—their teachers, coaches, and peers. A parent's role is not simply that of a police officer (especially the further you get into the teen years); it's moderator, counselor, and guide.

Your child's use of media, internet, and entertainment can provide you with a great opportunity to initiate conversations about values, wisdom, discernment, and choices. Be aware of what your child listens to and watches. Create safe venues to discuss your thoughts, feelings, and values related to the content. Make sure they have positive growing relationships with other adults that will tell them the same things you would. Don't let the negative voices of culture do all of the talking, particularly on potentially life-altering subjects.

HOME
YOUR HOME AS A THIRD PARTY VOICE

As we established earlier, these are seasons when it may seem like your teen is not listening to you and that your voice carries little to no weight. Parental reaction to this (and understandably so) is often to speak more forcefully. But—surprise!—the best way to get your voice heard is not necessarily to speak more loudly. We can step back and be a little more strategic.

Don't underestimate the power of your *home* as a third-party voice in the life of your child. The statistics on teen susceptibility to media /entertainment/internet influences are remarkably skewed when sorted in light of the home environment.[11] Teens who come from certain homes are more likely to emerge less negatively influenced by destructive cultural voices. These are homes where there is:

» positive communication about the messages and effects of media influence,

» a clearly articulated standard of behavior (what is right/wrong, acceptable/not),

» consistent fair consequences, and

» empowering versus controlling parenting.

What might that look like? Here are some ideas for how you can help monitor the technology and media voices in your teen's life and create a positive third-party voice in your home:

» Limit the number of hours and time of day that the TV and internet can be used (limit yourself, as well, if it's an issue. Practice what you preach!).

» Consider a "no computer use behind closed doors" policy. In our family, we have a rule that the internet is never used behind closed doors. This isn't to communicate distrust, but rather to create an atmosphere of openness and accountability.

» Teach your child to monitor his or her own media use (Remember, we're parenting for the launch. Soon they won't have you around to point out that they've been on the computer for three hours straight!).

» Make sure homework and other responsibilities are completed before TV, social media, and video gaming.

» Don't limit your efforts to the above behavior modifications. Make sure you talk about the messages your teen is hearing. When you hear questionable song lyrics that differ from your family's values, ask your teen what he/she thinks of them and why. (Pick up your kids' headphones once in awhile to see what they're listening to!)

» Do the same with TV and movie viewing. Encourage analytical and critical thinking instead of passive acceptance.

» Avoid simply making pronouncements about your own opinion and resist the urge to turn the conversation into a lecture. Ask good questions that promote discernment, evaluation of messages, and self-examination about your teen's own beliefs and values.

THEIR INNER VOICE (CONSCIENCE)

Your children may go on to achieve great success in college and an eventual career (and in other areas in life), but if they lack strong intrinsic values, those efforts could easily go up in smoke. At the very least, they could be severely compromised. Hopefully by the time they hit the teen years, they will have a well-developed inner sense of right and wrong—and an aversion to violating it.

In our parenting, we want to be doing more than simply policing behavior. We don't just want to control their decisions and get them to make choices that please us in the short-term. Trust me, if that's the end goal, when they leave your home (and your rules), they may go wild! They will only have learned to avoid punishment and conflict. They will not have learned to steer themselves toward wise choices led by strong inner convictions.

When your child violates a rule, do you simply punish the behavior? Or do you lead him or her into deeper conversations about the heart behind the behavior? Do you only seek to solve surface problems? Or do you seek to help your teens understand the deeper motivations (in themselves and in others) that create and exacerbate those problems? This recalls the old adage about whether you should hand a poor man a fish, or teach him to go fishing!

When one of our boys was in school, he was suspended from the bus for punching another student. Of course, we were shocked and upset (and frankly, more than a little irritated, because we had to drive him back and forth to school for a week!). He was, at first, defensive when we questioned him about it. As we probed deeper, however, to the heart attitude behind the behavior, we discovered what had precipitated it. As it turned out, the recipient of our son's blow had been bullying another student. (One thing we've discovered about this son is he has an extremely strong sense of justice. When that is violated, look out! Surprise, surprise, as of this writing, he's planning to become an attorney.)

Obviously, punching someone was not an appropriate reaction. However, if we'd simply left it at that level and punished the behavior without training the heart, we would have missed out on a very valuable opportunity. This situation provided us with the chance to train him in:

» recognizing his emotions "rising up" when he observes an injustice,
» understanding he doesn't have to be the one to administer justice; there are other avenues,
» communication,
» self-restraint, and
» forgiveness.

Through his teen years, it was heartening to see an inner voice developing in our son that helped regulate his behavior—not because he was afraid of getting into trouble, but because he wanted to do the right thing.

A good conscience will serve your teens well when they are out from under your supervision. Again, asking probing questions is a good way to help your teen develop self-awareness and a good conscience. So is exposing him to an objective standard of truth for establishing moral convictions.

Point out to your teen that a value is a belief system, guiding principle, or philosophy that determines your decisions, actions, and behaviors. These internal guiding principles motivate you and show others what is important to you. Your values are like a compass, pointing you in a consistent, honorable direction.

There is an emerging trend today toward "tolerance" that can make people afraid of drawing the line between right and wrong. Unfortunately, many have relaxed their values for fear of appearing judgmental. Because of this, some teens lack even an appropriate vocabulary to identify and articulate their convictions.

You may want to go through the following list of values descriptors with your teens, just to make sure you are on the same page. There is also an activity you can do with them, from the *What I Wish I Knew at 18 Student Guide*, to help facilitate the discussion.

Personal Values

Healthy living	Honesty
Self-discipline	Cleanliness
Fitness	Humor
Punctuality	Thankfulness
Integrity	Loyalty
Commitment	Industriousness
Trustworthiness	Faith
Obedience	Financial responsibility
Courage	Modesty
Purity	Reliability
Humility	Motivation

Social Values

Compassion	Generosity
Justice	Gratitude
Kindness	Courage
Forgiveness	Perseverance
Grace	Unconditional love
Flexibility	Contentment
Hospitality	Honor
Gentleness	Dignity
Morality	Respect
Faith	Courtesy
Patience	Teamwork

1. Have each family member explain which values are in the top five in each category, and why. Can you think of—and share with the group—examples of how these values affect (or should affect) your decision-making on a regular basis?

2. Role play – Act out the following scenarios, with each person acting our his or her response in the situation:

    Scenario #1 – A teacher ridicules a student's views on capital punishment (or other controversial topic)

    Scenario #2 – Someone has a job as a server in a restaurant. A co-worker urges him or her to pocket tips, rather than putting them in the common pool of tips for all the servers to divide at the end of the night, as policy requires.

    Scenario #3 – Someone at their lunch table in the cafeteria suggests "shunning" another student who is different/unliked for some reason

3. Use this as an opportunity to identify which are shared values in your family (e.g., cleanliness, punctuality, honesty) and which are more important to each of you as individuals (e.g., justice, compassion, etc.). If you completed a family mission statement back in Chapter Two, this would be a good time to take it out and go over it again. Here are some more ideas to keep the discussion rolling:

    » Are there ways that having similar values make you closer as a family or ways that conflicts over values create tension?

    » How have different family members handled situations in which their values and beliefs have been challenged, tested, or questioned?

    » Which are areas of personal preference or style, and which are non-negotiable moral and ethical issues for you?

YOUR VOICE IS MORE POWERFUL
THAN YOU KNOW

While your teen is most likely spending more time listening to other voices during this season (whether in person or online), they are *not* necessarily cutting ties or rejecting your ideals. In fact, many times what you may perceive as a rejection is not so much that as it is a re-negotiation of your former parent-child relationship. Perhaps what your teen isn't saying is "I'm rejecting you." Rather, he or she may be saying, "Hey, I'm almost grown up. It's time to cut a new deal," or "Give me some credit; I get it!" Whether we're talking about curfews or communication, what we want to avoid is burning our bridges.

This is your golden opportunity. Don't miss it. If you recognize and react to this new reality with trust and they handle it well, you have the opportunity to build an even greater platform for parental influence and relationship in your teen's life. This matured relationship can be a source of great benefit and pleasure to you both in the future.

Be encouraged. Statistics support the idea that, despite appearances to the contrary, parents are still the number one influencers in a young person's life. The majority of teenagers report that they have values and general beliefs similar to their parents and consider their parents as being highly significant in their lives.

Guaranteed: your children will make some not-so-great choices along with the good ones. They will stumble here and there as they make great strides. Sometimes, they will want you there to pick them up, dust them off and set them straight again. Other times, they'll prefer you keep your distance and let them handle it.

If you have the benefit of a variety of positive, encouraging, and healthy voices in your child's life, you'll be able to approach the launch with a greater sense of peace. He (or she) will be all the more prepared for the real world, where we all have to sort the good voices from the bad. Hopefully, they'll surround themselves with the good.

That's all part of the journey . . . and an important part of the road to adulthood.

TRY THIS

1. Consider having a "No Screen/No Tech Day" in your household once in a while. (This can be as difficult for parents as it is for teens!) Make an effort to lessen the influence of the technology and entertainment on all of you.

    What other activities can you do that will encourage time together, real conversations and interaction, and physical activity? Often the best conversations arise naturally as we do things together, as opposed to trying to force them. These are times when your "voice" is most likely to be heard and listened to.

2. Make a list of the five most influential people in your teen's life. Are you happy with the list? Whom would you like to add? Is there anyone about whom you have concerns? Discuss these with your spouse or parenting partner. Come up with some strategies for ensuring there are strong, positive third party voices in your teen's life.

3. Ask your teen to identify the top five people he or she admires most and why. What are the common denominators? The people they admire can be an indicator of your child's priorities and values. Do they align with your family values?

TAKE FIVE

1. How much airtime do other voices have in your household on a daily basis? Do you think and discuss their influences (both good and bad), or just passively accept their input? Think about friends, TV, internet, music, school, etc. Which are positive influences? Which may need to be scaled back and their influence diminished? How will you do this?

2. Think of particular books, movies, shows, or songs that reinforce the ideas and values you want to emphasize to your children. Consider how you might strategically arrange for them to be introduced—a family movie night, reading project, or "offhand suggestion?" These can be springboards to great conversations, or at least food for thought. Also, be on the alert for current celebrities, movies, music, etc. that DO send a positive message. Make sure you highlight these to your kids; knowing how influenced they are by pop culture, they're likely to take notice!

3. What do you think about the idea that "parenting is a team sport?" Who are other adults that you would consider to be on your "team?" If you need to shore this up, who are some likely candidates?

Part Three:

Transition Preparation

FROM DRIVER TO PASSENGER

LAUNCH TIME!

And, they're off! You're ready to release your teen into the "real world." Will he or she set the alarm, wash clothes, make the bed, study, handle the social adjustment, live within a budget, and stick with his or her values? How about *call home?*

The first three to six months after the launch are crucial and set the stage for the next four years. Getting off to a strong start is both a priority and an imperative!

To set you and your teen up for a successful transition, the next two chapters tackle: 1) the all-important shift from the driver's seat to the passenger seat and 2) the key ingredients to a strong start (while avoiding the most common mistakes young adults make at this crucial time).

Here's to a strong and healthy transition with lots of momentum for the future!

CHAPTER NINE

MOVING FROM DRIVER TO PASSENGER

*The most important thing that parents can teach
their children is how to get along without them.*
Frank A. Clark

I (Arlyn) remember the first time I heard the term "helicopter parent." It was at my daughter's college freshman orientation, where they separated parents and students into different rooms and gave us each a good talking-to. There they told us, in no uncertain terms, that *helicopter parenting* would be detrimental to our students' success in college.

They didn't have to explain what they were talking about, even though I'd never heard the phrase before that day. I knew exactly what it meant!

Can't you just see it? A young adult is off to the real world—college or the work force—ready to make his or her mark in life. As he does, there is a helicopter hovering over him, the pilot barking advice through a megaphone. The copter sweeps in for closer views at times. Other times, it pulls away slightly but it is always a very real presence.

Our children's generation has seen the rise of helicopter parents more than any other. Helicopter parents are always there (emotionally if not physically and not always in a good way). They hover. At their worst, they are always advising and intervening, enabling and rescuing, offering opinions and sometimes outright manipulating. Why? Generally speaking, the reasons include "to be involved in my child's life," to "help," and to "be an advocate." Good intentions—but when they start to work against our ultimate parenting objectives, these efforts can actually become counterproductive and downright detrimental.

"Millennials have had helicopter parents who have protected them," says Dan Jones, president of the Association for University and College Counseling Center Directors and the director of counseling and psychological services at Appalachian State University in Boone, N.C. "They haven't had the opportunity to struggle. When they come to college and bad things happen, they haven't developed resiliency and self-soothing skills."[12]

Let's back up and identify why this is such a problem today, since our parents' generation didn't suffer from it as much. Theirs was (again, generally speaking) more a generation of self-sufficiency—of parents and their adult children living their own lives. This, however, is the generation of highly involved parenting. This is the generation whose fathers are in the Lamaze classes and the delivery rooms, whose parents are at every ball practice, and some of whose moms (or dads) give up lucrative careers to take on the full-time career of parenting. And, they give it every bit as much effort and excellence as their corporate careers!

These involved parents serve on the committees at the preschool and bring cupcakes to every party.

They attend every soccer practice and ballet class.

They make their kids' beds and pick up after them.

They sometimes DO their kids' homework!

They advocate for their children at teacher conferences and school board meetings. They regularly call and email the teachers and school board (often to the *extreme*, teachers tell us!).

They make every personal effort they can to help their kids make the team, earn a 4.0, get the job . . .

So, guess who's having a little trouble letting go when Junior goes off to the real world?

(Hint: It's not Junior!)

FROM DIRECTOR TO CHIEF ENCOURAGER

I don't like to see anyone trip and fall, much less my children. That being said, if I'd loaded them up with full body armor throughout their growing up years, they wouldn't have experienced much of life, would they? Nor would they be well-prepared for life on their own.

We had some friends who used to make their five-year old wear protective gear when he rode his bicycle. We're not just talking a helmet here—they outfitted him from head to toe: helmet, elbow pads, gloves, and knee-pads. The poor little guy could hardly walk, much less learn to ride a bicycle!

Needless to say, his parents' overprotectiveness worked against their objective. Their helicopter parenting style prevented their son from accomplishing the very thing they were (supposedly) working toward. The boy did, eventually, learn to ride a bike—after the parents relaxed a bit and gave him some freedom. A helmet was perfectly sufficient protection. Sure, he probably sustained a few scrapes and bruises in the process. But isn't that how we all learn to navigate life?

Young children need their parents A LOT. They need us to interpret the world for them, help them make decisions, recognize and avoid danger, choose the right kinds of friends, and know when to work and when to play. That being said, our role is an evolving one. In fact, our goal should be to work ourselves *out* of a job!

When our kids were little, we put training wheels on their bikes, and then took them off as they demonstrated increased strength, balance, and confidence. That's how we should be approaching the launch. We go from holding them on the bike with both hands, to keeping one hand on the seat, to letting them ride alone with training wheels, to taking off the training wheels and cheering like crazy from the sidelines. That's what being a "chief encourager" is all about (emphasis on the *sidelines*).

Going from director to chief encourager is one of the biggest challenges for parents during the years leading up to and including the launch. And truthfully, it can be a big challenge for teens as well (although they probably won't admit it). Change isn't easy for any of us. But if teens are going to be successful, confident adults, they need to be able to operate independently. The test of your good parenting will be how well they can do all the things you trained them to do—without your reminding them. And the time to start practicing, if you haven't already, is *now*.

INCREMENTALLY RELEASE CONTROL

You may be wondering if we're going to get to the topic of discipline. You may be encountering tension and conflict in your relationship with your teen and are looking for ways to tighten the reins to gain some control (and ostensibly some sanity) in the situation.

If lack of discipline has been the issue, tightening the reins is not likely going to be your answer, or at least not your only answer. So, to clarify the objective of *this* book, we are assuming that you *have* been disciplining your child up to this point. If all hell has broken loose at your house and there is no control whatsoever, then there are likely some other books you will want to read alongside this one that can help you get control.

We want to focus here on how to *relinquish* control. Since you have chosen to read this particular book, it's probably safe to say you are at least a moderately active parent who is interested in the best outcome for your children. We are assuming you have taught them right from wrong, established a measure of responsibility, maintained at least some degree of accountability, set goals for the future, and have a set of standards with which you expect your kids to comply.

As we approach the launch we should be increasingly *handing over* the reins, not tightening them. That's not to say we throw our teens the reins when they're sixteen and say, "Have at it, kid; you're on your own!" But, to carry the horse analogy a little further, it does mean we start to loosen the reins a bit and give the horse its head, as they say in the equestrian world. It means letting teens start making decisions and having more freedom to do and say and think and be . . . on their own . . . even if they have some failures along the way.

Wouldn't you rather have a horse that can find its way back to the barn on its own, as opposed to one that has no sense of direction unless it's wearing a bridle and reined by a strong hand?

For consummate perfectionists (or those whose own identity and self-worth are largely caught up in how their children perform), this can be difficult. Your kids won't be perfect and they will more likely than not fail at some things. The key is to start with little things, so when they do stumble the fall won't be as hard as later on, when there's more at stake. For example, in the high school years:

> » If they sleep in, don't nag and yell to get them out of bed. Don't be quick to write them a note excusing their tardiness. Yes, it may affect their grade if this habit gets out of hand. Hopefully they'll get a handle on it after they have to serve lunch duty in the cafeteria a few times (that's how it works at our kids' school)!
>
> » If they choose to spend all their money on clothes and food, let them. Then when they're sitting home Friday night, while all their friends are at the movies, because they didn't budget properly, so be it. Don't bail them out! That's real life. Hopefully they will think twice before they overspend again.
>
> » If they fill their calendar with social engagements and leave school assignments to the last minute, don't run them up to the store at 10:00 p.m. for poster board for that project that's due tomorrow morning. Again, this may affect their grade, but they need to feel the weight of it.
>
> » If they are having a conflict with another student at school, or even a teacher, don't jump in and try to fix it. Talk about how they can solve the problem themselves. Do they need to make an appointment to talk with the teacher? A counselor? A mediator? Encourage them to problem-solve themselves.

Don't try to fix everything for them, or rush to give them the answers they need quickly. It's tempting to intervene or respond immediately for the sake of efficiency, or to do damage control, but it will only delay their independence and maturity. The busier we are, the more likely we are to just tell them what to do or do it for them, but it's a short-term gain and a long-term loss.

IT'S THEIR LIFE

I find it painful to watch the popular reality show about a group of stage moms who are overly obsessed with their young daughters' dance careers (some as young as five). The mothers rant, scream, cry and generally terrorize their daughters, the dance coaches, and each other. Why? Because they have a dream for their daughters that may or may not be shared by the girls themselves. Sadly, this is not at all uncommon—parents living vicariously through their children, forcing their children to live out *their* (the parents') dreams.

On a recent visit to a Nashville restaurant, we met a delightful server we'll call Katie. We were talking with her about the music scene in Nashville and another server made a side comment that Katie had a lot of talent she wasn't using. When we asked her about it, Katie admitted she had come to Nashville to attend college as a music major. She told us she had graduated in that field and was an accomplished blues performer, but was currently pursuing a career in criminal justice and doing nothing with her music—not even casually.

When we asked her why, she told us her mother had pushed her relentlessly in voice and piano lessons from age four. "My Katie is going to be a star," her mother would proclaim to anyone and everyone.

Katie said dryly, "I certainly had no desire to be a *star*. That was her deal."

When all of us expressed dismay that she was not using her talents, she brushed us off. "I was forced to perform so much as a child, " she said emphatically, "I don't want to give my mother the satisfaction of *ever* seeing me perform again."

Wow! How sad. What is the world missing out on—and what is Katie missing out on—because of her (understandable) reaction to her mother's pressure?

Our kids need to know that their worth is based on themselves, not on their performance or their accomplishments. After all, it's *their* life.

Maybe your son doesn't want the pressure of attending an Ivy League school. It's *his* life. Maybe a daughter doesn't want to be first chair in the symphony and doesn't want to practice her violin three hours a day. It's *her* life. Maybe a child wants to be an artist instead of an attorney. A designer, not a doctor. Let them live their lives, with affirmation. Don't withhold your praise and affection because they're not doing exactly what you want them to do or how you want them to do it.

One of the greatest gifts we can give our kids is a blessing and one of the most destructive things we can do is withhold one. Remember, it's about wings, not strings. That means allowing them to live their dream.

A SPECIAL NOTE TO MOMS

My husband is the youngest of six children, and I remember my late mother-in-law having a tough time when he left for Marine Corps boot camp at age 18. In his haste, he forgot some record albums, leaving them scattered on the floor by the stereo, and a pair of his shoes in the middle of the family room floor. I think she left them there for three months! Bless her heart; she wasn't quite ready to admit her nest was really empty.

While having a child leave home can produce feelings of loss in both dads and moms, it's generally moms who feel it most, particularly as it relates to their own role and identity. More often than not (and I realize there are exceptions) it is mothers who are the front line nurturers. Whether they work outside the home or not, they still tend to be the ones who are the primary day-to-day caregivers in the first 18 years. Because of this, they often experience the strongest sense of loss.

If the child you are launching is your last or only, you may have the double whammy of experiencing the "empty nest." *Empty nest syndrome* is a psychological condition that generally affects women, producing feelings of loss and/or grief when one or more of their children leave home. If a woman has placed her primary personal identity on her role as a mother, then the finality of her children leaving home can be especially traumatic.

If you find yourself feeling weepy, regretful, panicked, and perhaps even angry, it's vital to allow yourself the necessary time to work through the loss and adjust to your new normal. However, if the feelings become overwhelming or obsessive, or if your anxiety starts turning into behaviors that affect your child who is now living away from home for the first time, watch out!

It happens all the time, especially when a mom has been pouring so much of her own identity into her role as mother. Letting her grown children go and giving them wings can seem like losing her very "self." We see this manifested in so many different ways—coddling, doing too much for them, crying, saying things like, "My baby is leaving . . . "

No, your *baby* is not leaving.

Please don't say this in front of your kids. If that's how you feel as a parent (your young adult is not your "baby"), you are going to be subliminally messaging that. You're essentially communicating that you don't want them to go, you still want them around underfoot, depending on you. This can influence their decision where to go next, and how well they will do when they get there. At the very least, it can create unnecessary and undeserved guilt. Bottom line, this kind of behavior is just another form of *strings* and often results in young adults who are:

» insecure about leaving/navigating new environments,

» fearful,

» hesitant,
» lacking confidence,
» lacking motivation, and/or
» ultimately resentful.

In the end, we want our young adults to believe in themselves and to know their parents believe in them, too. I (Arlyn), as of this writing, have launched four children and have one left to go. I do understand how it feels, as a mom, to let them go.

I want to encourage you mothers reading this to give your kids freedom to grow—and start enjoying some freedom yourself! If you are struggling with the thought of losing your identity as your child moves into this next (independent) season of life, keep in mind that YOU are much more than just your child(ren)'s mom! In fact, here are some things you can do to move forward with excitement and confidence as it relates to your own personal development and as it relates to a new level of relationship with your adult child.

» If you are grieving, acknowledge it, don't stuff it. Putting on a happy face and not dealing with your real emotions will only cause further problems down the line, emotionally and physically. You don't have to tell everyone how you're feeling, but do tell those closest to you.

» Find some positives about the new situation and actively take advantage of them. Do you now have an empty bedroom you can redecorate and turn into another kind of useful space like an office, craft room, or guest room? Do you have more time in your schedule now that you can use to go back to school or do something you've been itching to do? Is there a career (or career change) in your future, a hobby you've wanted to start, or a volunteer opportunity at a local charity?

» Treat yourself! Moms often put themselves last in priority. Put yourself first for a change! Treat yourself to a manicure or pedicure, go out to dinner or a movie with your spouse or friends, get a massage . . . do something special for *yourself* for a change.

» Build new friendships or renew old ones. The ability to spend more time with friends is a great *benefit* of your transition from full-time parent to parent-with-kids-launched.

» Spend some time with yourself! If you've been a busy mom, being "alone" more will be a novelty. "What will I do with myself?" you may wonder. This is a good time to get to know yourself again. It may be a good time for prayer and journaling, as well.

» Set new goals and dream new dreams. You now have the capacity and freedom to expand your horizons.

» Schedule regular times for phone calls (decide these in advance) and don't inundate him or her with calls, texts, or Facebook messages. And, don't let yourself feel the loss all over again if your child fails to reply as frequently as he or she once did to your calls or texts. Young adults are experiencing so many new things, and they likely have a busy schedule and many demands. Don't take it personally. This is part of their own adjustment—getting settled into their new surroundings, relationships, and responsibilities.

» Resist the urge to emphasize your loss to your son or daughter. It can cause guilt and come across as being needy and manipulative (even though that's not your intention). Try to communicate in a positive, unemotional, and empowering way, despite your own feelings.

One of the best things I think Doug and I have done with our launches has been to view them as adventures for our kids and for us. They were going through their own sense of loss and anxiety, too, even if they didn't show it. I believe our strength helped them be strong, too. Sure, there were a few moments of tears. The little people they were are gone forever, only living on in our photographs and memories. Oh, how I loved being the mom of those little people!

But, I also love being the mom of big people—and I'm sure you will, too.

SET THEM UP FOR WISE DECISION-MAKING

The teen years include many decisions that can have a significant impact on a child's future. However, if we make all their decisions *for* them, we can potentially do more harm than good. Making wise decisions is something teens and young adults must learn to do if they're going to be successful on their own.

For example, Doug and I have allowed our children to choose their own high school and college classes, with discussion but very little interference from us. We talked with them about their objectives and options, but pretty much left the final decisions up to them. We have no regrets about that.

Do you know what happens when a person is overly managed, whether by a parent, a spouse, or an employer—or by anyone else, for that matter? The closer the relationship, the greater the collateral damage. One result is they become increasingly less able to make their own decisions. They're always looking over their shoulder, in fear, hesitation, or in debilitating servitude. They struggle to make even the smallest decisions, from what-do-I-have-for-dinner to what-should-be-my-college-major. Like a weak muscle that never gets exercised, their decision-making ability atrophies.

The other possible (and frequent) result is they rebel. They go off the deep end in the opposite direction because they can't stand the feeling of anyone giving *any* input into their life. I can't tell you how many young adults I've seen who've been tightly controlled or overly sheltered right up to the minute they left home, who go crazy when they get to college. Many of them make terrible, life-altering decisions that derail their future plans because they've never been trusted to make their own choices.

Do you want to set your teen up for wise decision-making? Before offering your own opinion about their decisions, ask them to give you their own thoughts first. Let them start by telling you what decision they would make if you let them. Then, as you hear them articulate wise choices and sound reasoning, you can start to trust them to actually decide. Also, take every opportunity to invite them into your own decision-making and let them be part of the process. Teach them the following steps to making good decisions (From *What I Wish I Knew at 18*):[13]

Step 1: Determine your key decision criteria. Identify the key factors in making your decision. For example, when determining which college to attend, people consider a number of criteria, such as reputation, size, location, available majors, tuition costs, etc. It's especially helpful if you can prioritize your criteria from most to least important.

Step 2: Get the facts. Gather all of the facts about your decision options that you can, along with any accompanying assumptions. In some cases, you'll have to use your best guess.

Step 3: Identify all of your alternatives. Here, you'll want to consider all realistic options without prejudging. Be thinking, "No choice is a bad choice," at this stage.

Step 4: Engage wise counsel. Solicit the views of experienced and insightful people who know you well and understand the decision at hand. This is an especially important step when a teen is considering different careers or college majors. It really pays to hear from actual practitioners in the fields he or she is exploring. And, if you're a person of faith, pray for wisdom and guidance.

Step 5: Conduct an objective pro/con analysis for each option. Now that you have the facts and some quality opinions from people you respect, you're in a position to develop pro/con analyses for each option based on your key decision criteria. Here, you record the advantages and disadvantages and weigh them by importance. This is a particularly valuable step for visual learners, since the right decision often emerges when the pros significantly outweigh the cons.

Step 6: Consider your "gut instinct" or intuition. Chances are, by the time you've completed the fifth step, your best choice will have emerged. However, the final test is what your intuition is telling you. If, after completing steps one to five, you have a nagging feeling that it isn't right, sleep on it. If you're still uncertain the following day, have a heart-to-heart talk with yourself and your most trusted advisors. This will either reinforce your preliminary decision (which will provide the needed conviction) or it will compel you to more seriously consider your other alternatives.

Don't, under any circumstances, forget this final step. It may make all the difference in the world!

DON'T RESCUE THEM (TOO QUICKLY)

Of course, if our children are ever in any real danger or distress, we will want to offer assistance. Our teens and young adults should always feel safe and comfortable coming to us for help, if they get into a difficult spot. My parents were wonderful at achieving the perfect balance of freedom to fail and support when I did. However, we don't want to swoop in too quickly or too thoroughly. Sometimes falling flat on their faces is exactly what they need—including facing the consequences of bad decisions.

Here's a snapshot of what can happen when a child is consistently rescued by his or her parents. When two of my children were in high school, they were (understandably) exasperated by an incident involving their classmates. Two boys had been out drinking on a weekend. In the middle of the night, they stole a car belonging to another friend's parents, crashed it into a tree, and fled the scene. They went home to their own beds and never said a word to anyone.

Eventually, word got out who had done it, though there was never any formal investigation or charges filed. The parents of the boy who had been driving settled with the owners of the car and the case never saw the (legal) light of day.

The interesting thing to me was my kids' (18 and 15 at the time) reaction.

"Mom, that kid's parents have been bailing him out since elementary school. Whenever he gets into trouble at school, his mom goes in and yells at the teacher and principal and he gets away with it every time! This time is no different."

I don't think any of us have to wonder how that young man will fare in the real world. He has never had to face up to the weight of his own (bad) decisions and, therefore, has not developed the character he will need to successfully navigate environments with increased responsibility, such as college, career, and family. His parents will eventually wish they had helped him learn those lessons when the stakes weren't so high.

The children of rescuing and enabling parents have trouble making sound decisions as adults. They often fail to understand the correlation between their actions and the consequences. They lack the necessary soft skills to succeed in college and the work force—things like initiative, discipline, integrity, perseverance, respect, and patience.

When we fail to exercise a muscle, it becomes weak and cannot support the desired actions of the body. When we as parents fail to relinquish control—when we helicopter, overprotect, over-advocate, rescue, and enable—we do the same to our children. They become weak in areas where they need to be strong, because we exercised our own "muscles" in those situations and not theirs.

Some good friends of ours had to work through this when they were called in on a parent-teacher conference with Mrs. Thompson, their daughter Megan's math teacher. Mrs. Thompson was concerned about Megan's poor record of homework completion and even more concerned about her socializing and lack of respect in class. Our friends chose to sit quietly as Mrs. Thompson leveled her complaints against Megan, without interrupting or defending her. When the teacher was finished her presentation of the facts as she saw them, they asked Megan if she had anything to say for herself. She didn't. It was all true. Our friends expressed their support for Mrs. Thompson, asked Megan to apologize, and assured her of their commitment to follow up at home with consequences and accountability for Megan. They did.

While it was certainly an unpleasant situation, it was a wake-up call for Megan, who didn't realize how her disrespect had personally hurt the teacher. There was a distinct turnaround in her behavior—and she managed to come out of the class with a B! Mrs. Thompson later told our friends how much she appreciated their cooperation—and that, in her experience, that kind of parental follow-through was the exception and not the norm. Most parents, she said, would have defended their daughter and the problem would have continued unchecked.

When parents do that in front of their children, they demonstrate disrespect and undermine authority. Those are terrible things to teach kids. No wonder our kids are having so many problems in the workplace after graduation!

The teachers we meet in our work with *What I Wish I Knew at 18* routinely lament this growing and extremely frustrating trend. In generations past, parents customarily viewed teachers as allies and, if a child got in trouble at school, it was "Look out!" at home. Many times these days, the opposite is true. If a child misbehaves at school and the teacher has to send a message home, or call a parent-teacher conference, a parent will come in on the warpath—against the teacher, not the student! This is yet another by-product of performance and child-centered parenting. Sadly, these parents are intervening and defending rather than training and empowering their kids through letting them face the consequences of their poor behavior.

It's contributing to the "entitlement mentality" we hear all too often as a descriptor of the attitude of today's younger generation. Not surprisingly, it's one of the most common complaints (and career destroyers!) we hear from employers. And, it all begins in the home with parents enabling and staying in the driver's seat.

As they say in the popular TV commercial, *Don't be that guy.*

SET A GREAT EXAMPLE

That quote, "Children do what you *do*, not what you *say*," is brilliant. So true!

Parental integrity is a huge factor in whether a teen's transition to the real world goes smoothly or not. It's crucial that they see you personally applying to your own life the principles you are telling them to apply to theirs.

Our family happens to be a praying family. That's not to say everyone has to be, but that's a part of our daily life. We try to eat dinner together every night, and we always pray before the meal.

One of the reasons we do this is because we legitimately believe that when we say our thanks out loud—and ask for divine help and guidance with our concerns—it makes a real difference. The second reason we pray together with our kids is that we want them to be praying people. How reasonable would it be to expect them to be persons of faith if they never saw us exercising ours?

We try to be similarly open in other areas of our life, and endeavor to lead by example. Whether it's matters of faith or finances, or anything else, we hope our teens and adult children see us living life with transparency, humility, and integrity. When they can, it makes it more likely that they will follow in our footsteps, as we move to the passenger seat.

Take a moment for a self-check. Consider the following arenas and assess the degree to which what you *say* lines up with what you *practice*:

» How you talk about other people when they're not present
» The kind of language you use
» Servanthood/volunteering/charity
» Giving

- » Physical health/nutrition/exercise
- » Tobacco and alcohol use
- » Viewing habits (media/online/movies/TV)
- » Relationships (commitment, respect, honor, forgiveness, faithfulness)
- » Honesty
- » Work ethic
- » Faith
- » Finances

I knew one family who had significant issues with their two teen boys and the way they treated one of their parents. The boys spoke disrespectfully, were critical and sarcastic, and lived with an attitude of entitlement. The parents were understandably upset by the situation.

After spending some time in their home, however, I quickly became aware of the real origin of the problem. One of the parents treated the other in the same ways the boys were behaving! These boys were only acting out what had been modeled for them—and the offending parent was completely blind to it.

Walking *our* talk makes it more likely that when they leave home, they will walk *theirs*.

START TREATING THEM LIKE (REAL) GROWN UPS

"You treat me like a kid."

"Because you act like one!"

Have you ever had that conversation at your house? Teens are constantly and increasingly tugging at the reins, wanting more and more slack. Usually a parent's next response is, "When you deserve it, I'll give it to you."

When teens ask to be treated like adults, what they're really wanting are the *privileges* of adulthood. A car. Money in their pocket. Decision-making authority. Unfortunately, because of the nature of childhood (immaturity) and the proclivity of some parents to demand perfection or performance—or to rescue, pamper, and enable—that day never comes, or doesn't come soon enough.

The reality is most teens are ready for more responsibility than we give them and are in need of opportunities to exercise it in matters big and small. Adults have extra rights and privileges that kids look forward to enjoying and usually want *now*. But remember that for adults, those privileges are usually attached to responsibility. For example:

1. I have a car (privilege). I must earn money to put gas in it and pay the insurance and maintenance (responsibility).

2. I live in a nice home (privilege). Again, I must earn an income to pay for it. I must clean and maintain it in order to keep it comfortable and in good repair (responsibility).

3. I work in a career that I love (privilege). To get here, I had to go through a number of years of education, training, and "paying my dues" at lower level positions. I still put in a great deal of effort on a daily basis, to meet my clients' expectations and deliver quality work (responsibility).

4. I can stay up (or out) as late as I want to, every night (privilege). However, I have children who like me to see them off to school early in the mornings, and a busy daily schedule of appointments and tasks that require me to have adequate sleep in order to be in top form (responsibility).

5. I can make any decision I want to (privilege). However, I have a spouse and children and grandchildren whose lives and happiness are influenced by my decisions (not to mention extended family, friends, colleagues, and neighbors). If I want to maintain relationships and respect from others, I need to keep them in mind when I make my own decisions. Sometimes, what I want to do is outweighed by what honors and benefits others (responsibility).

Do you see how these privileges have responsibilities attached to them? The immaturity of childhood looks at the privileges and says, "I want that! You need to treat me like an adult." What they need to understand is that privileges, in the real world, are attached to *responsibilities*. If we give them the privileges, but don't require them to live up to responsibilities, we set them up for an entitlement mentality—and for struggles in the real world.

As of this writing, the current teen jobless rate in the United States is nearly the highest ever. Is that because there are fewer jobs? To some extent. We're witnessing a plethora of older job candidates because of financial difficulties and other reasons. Many employers prefer to hire these older applicants because so many young people today fail to demonstrate the responsibility, reliability, social skills, and work ethic necessary to succeed on the job.

Colleges are reporting similar issues. In our work with *What I Wish I Knew at 18*, we talk to university presidents, advisors, and professors. They all echo, "So many students come to us poorly equipped with the work ethic and/or life skills required to be successful at the university level. Many of them have hardly had a responsibility in their life and have no idea what hard work is." I am paraphrasing, but it's a common complaint, backed up by statistics. As mentioned earlier, the United States ranked ninth in college enrollment and dead last in college completion.

If we want to launch our children well in the real world, they'd better go in knowing how to perform the responsibilities and exhibit the endurance and perseverance necessary to succeed and to earn the privileges they desire. That's real life

So, the next time your teen tells you he or she wants to be treated like an adult, do it! Treat him or her like a *real* adult—not just with privileges, though. Make sure there are responsibilities to go with them. Being an adult is hard work. Teens need to feel the weight of hard work incrementally, so when they hit the real world they can step into it gracefully instead of doing a crash and burn. By the way they respond, you can determine if they are ready for more responsibility and new boundaries.

You don't need to give up full control all at once. But you can start by requiring them to do things like:

» Contribute to their own income by getting a job (or babysitting, etc.).

» Manage their own money (If you contribute to their income, you can set them up with a bank account into which you make deposits. Have them budget their expenses and, if there's too much month left at the end of the money, that's a lesson well-learned for next month!).

» Buy their own car (or make a significant contribution to it).

» Do or pay for their own car maintenance. If they don't pay for it, require them to take the car in themselves for repairs. If they're borrowing your car, require them to fill it with gas at least once in a while, so they make the connection between car use and money spent.

» Make their own appointments (dentist, doctor, hair, etc.). Encourage them, as much as is appropriate and realistic, to go to the appointment themselves, fill out the paperwork, etc. (This works better for haircuts and check ups than for things like having wisdom teeth removed. Use your judgment here.).

» Keep track of their own calendar of appointments, schedules, deadlines, events, etc. without your constant reminders.

» Do their own laundry.

» Make some of the family meals (and prepare food for themselves when they're hungry).

» Clean up the house before and after they entertain friends.

Granted, directing them rather than empowering them can be easier and more efficient in the short-term and less messy than delegating and building self-sufficiency. Giving them what they want instead of going through the hassle of making them earn it can also seem simpler (and sure, it's fun to make our kids happy). However, it can be counterproductive in the long run.

If you are a parent who draws a great deal of identity and personal fulfillment from doing things for your children, it can be difficult to change your habits. You may feel like you're being mean. You may think things won't be done to your standards (and they probably won't!). But, if you want to set them up well for the launch and equip them to be happy, healthy, functioning, and successful adults, it *must* happen. It will pay huge dividends in the long run to start moving *now* to the passenger seat and becoming more of a cheerleader/coach as your teen learns to operate in the driver's seat of his or her life.

TAKE FIVE

How are you doing with the transition? Have you started moving from driver's to passenger seat? What are ways that you have been incrementally releasing control and empowering your children to make more of their own decisions and assume greater responsibility? If this has not been happening, when and in what areas will you start?

CHAPTER TEN

LAUNCH TIME!

*There isn't a child who hasn't gone out into the brave
new world who eventually doesn't return to the old
homestead carrying a bundle of dirty clothes.*
Art Buchwald

I (Dennis) was completely unprepared for the unpredictable waves of emotion and reflection, when it was time for our first launch. The ball started rolling when we began our college tours. It was the first time Jeanne and I envisioned Michael on his own in a different setting. I closely observed the other students on campus, who looked so much older. Or, did they? In two short years, he'd be just like them.

Then came the college applications. The seemingly endless college apps. As strange as it seems, I actually enjoyed reviewing Michael's essays. They gave me an opportunity to share my perspectives of his assets and value. But, because it was part of a "project," it only gave me a glimpse of the emotions I would soon be feeling.

Next were the graduation pictures. No problem, as we watched from a distance, the photographer working her magic. Then a few weeks later, we received an email containing the proofs, accompanied by this strangely melancholy background music. As I reviewed the images, I came across one that hit me like a lightning bolt. It captured everything that was good about Michael in a way I can't possibly describe—including the reality that he was now a young man. Mr. Tough Guy was turning into a softie.

Shortly before Michael left for college, I began reflecting on how I had done as his father. As I mentioned earlier, I recorded a list of "life success pointers" to share with him, which eventually became *What I Wish I Knew at 18*. I shared some of the pointers with him during those waning days, but the launch date came all too quickly and we didn't get to cover them all—at least not then. Before we knew it, we were headed to Malibu and Pepperdine University.

After a two-day orientation program, we said our goodbyes (or, in my case, simply "Thanks," was all that came out), and we were dismissed. He stayed behind to begin his new life chapter, as we headed back to the car in silence—each taking in all that had just happened and processing it in our own ways. I'll never forget it.

Life would never be the same for us or for him . . . but it would still be great. Just different—the way it should be.

FOUR BIG CHANGES

At launch time, we practically and emotionally hand over the reins and transition to a new stage. It hits us all differently, because we—and our children—are unique. We're older and wiser, and now our role is changing. How well we handle this stage will have a major bearing on the quality of our parent-child relationship for years to come.

When teens reach the launch stage (roughly the year before and few years after leaving home—usually 17-20), they are embarking on a new life phase that is vitally important to their future. Because they're one part child and one part adult and maturity levels vary, some transition better than others. How well their parents handle it plays a crucial role, too.

What are some of the major changes our teens face as they enter adulthood?

1. *They're in the driver's seat now.* Their parents are transitioning into the passenger's seat and life will never be the same. It's a time of mixed emotions for them (as it is with us), because their

childhood is fading into the past and they're starting to take charge of the rest of their life, headed toward an uncertain future. It is often a strange brew of melancholy or nostalgia for what is lost and excitement for what might become. Is it any wonder our children often get more quiet and contemplative at this time? They're processing an incredible amount of change. Accordingly, we parents need to be especially understanding and encouraging at this stage.

2. *Major life decisions are awaiting them.* As if it's not enough to deal with the transition to the driver's seat, there's very little time before they make key decisions that will set the tone for the rest of their lives. Their decisions regarding college (where and what major) and career (or service) will position them on their pathway to independence. They'll learn to manage their finances, develop important disciplines, and perhaps meet the person of their dreams. It all adds up to *pressure*, because these decisions are far more important than those they've made before. It's a BIG gulp! So, they'll need to think strategically in a world that tells them to live in the moment.

3. *Life becomes increasingly competitive.* Over the last few decades, we've witnessed the "self esteem movement" where seemingly everyone gets a prize. Is it any wonder, then, that so many young adults are having difficulty handling the increasingly competitive landscape in the job market? Whether it's not being accepted into the college of their choice, or not landing their dream job, they'll soon come to realize that life isn't always fair. For instance, they must learn to build a winning competitive edge and persuasively market themselves to fulfill their career dreams. Or, they may need to take an entry-level position just to get their foot in the door. Regardless, they need to take control of these decisions and learn

to compete. Increasingly, their personal initiative will make or break their future.

4. *Their ability to form new, healthy friendships will be key.* The social transition to college is arguably among the most significant change people experience in life, although it is only the first of a series of transitions. As our economy globalizes and becomes more service-oriented, our workforces have become much more mobile. Change has now become a constant. So, in addition to leaving for college (I attended three), people are increasingly relocating to new communities, workplaces, and environments. We're no longer working for the same employers in the same location for extended periods of time, as in the past. This has huge social implications and places a premium on our ability to cultivate new and healthy friendships along the way. Some young adults are socially and relationally better at handling this than others.

WHAT THEY NEED FROM US

Clearly, all this change signals a significant transition for young adults and their parents. Because we parents have lived through this stage before (in our own time and situations), we're in a special position to share and encourage with empathy and understanding. In order to accomplish a successful launch, we need to provide them with:

» our unconditional love and understanding,
» our belief and encouragement,
» preparation and practical wisdom,
» our perspective of their uniqueness and value,
» full acknowledgement that it's their life and their dreams, not ours,
» a healthy and enduring relationship based on trust,
» an open door 24-7, and
» realistic expectations.

Now, imagine yourself in their shoes. Wouldn't the above list be ideal? By offering them, we can be that much more assured that our young adults will continue to invite us into their world. It can pave the way for a new kind of relationship in the years ahead.

PHASE ONE: THE LATE HIGH SCHOOL YEARS

As students progress through their junior and senior years of high school, they start tasting life as an adult. The first milestone comes with the driver's license and all the associated *responsibility* (and parental stress!). For many unsuspecting parents, this begins the transition phase as their teens spend an increasing amount of time away from home. Ours sure did! Teens love the freedom and mobility that comes with those car keys, and most parents soon notice an abrupt decline in available time with them.

Then along come the various "next step" programs in schools. Life readiness courses involving college prep, career planning, personal finance, family/consumer science, and life skills are now a part of their curricular menu (or if not, they should be). The college/career search begins in earnest, involving campus visits, aptitude testing for admissions, and choosing the key college selection criteria. (Parents also experience the joy of completing financial aid applications and the FAFSA, but that's another story.)

Will they take a year off? Will they join the military? Will they go straight to the workforce? Their first part-time job may become full-time, which, perhaps more than anything else, brings home the reality that their world is changing.

These years offer parents great opportunities to guide their teens while loosening the reins. College and scholarship applications may be the first experience for your son or daughter to market himself or herself, and for most, this doesn't come naturally. By coming alongside your teens, as they share their stories and competitive strengths on the applications, you'll have a natural avenue to offer what you think makes them special. Have them write the first drafts and offer to review them. It's a great chance to get out the personal balance sheet you wrote up in Chapter Six, affirming their strengths and revealing ones they've missed. And, it's a great relationship capital builder!

Finally comes the college decision itself. Since every family situation is unique, it's difficult to generalize about this, but here are some pointers we've found helpful:

» Where possible, allow your teen as much influence as you can on the final selection.

» Share all of your perspectives together and let them analyze the choices and convey their wishes.

» Listen to their hopes and dreams, even though financial and other considerations may ultimately be a factor.

» Help them explore creative ideas to help pay for college or trade school. Don't let financial concerns scare them (or you) away from pursuing the dream of post-secondary education. Money does matter, but don't overlook the ways it may be possible.

» Remember that this is a decision where mutual understanding is critical.

» For those who opt for a different route (e.g., workforce, military, community service, and missions), parents can be an invaluable asset during this transition, as well. These young adults may be living on their own or in a community, but they'll need some guidance for managing finances, establishing a household, buying necessary furnishings and a car, and the like.

Soon, you'll be having more "adult" conversations than you ever imagined. They will quickly realize how much they took your care for granted and will appreciate your practical wisdom for their new start in life.

THE SUMMER BEFORE—A RITE OF PASSAGE

This season will pass in a nanosecond. Whether they have summer jobs or not, your just-graduated teen WILL naturally want to spend more time with friends. After all, soon they'll all be scattered to the four winds, all navigating their new lives and environments. They are increasingly feeling this impending sense of loss, so fun with friends is their preferred antidote. Don't take it personally when you play second fiddle. They've got a lot on their minds.

The summer before launch time offers you wonderful opportunities to solidify your bond for the years ahead. Here are some ideas for you to consider that will build a platform to support the phase of parenting:

» *Develop a blessing packet.* One of the greatest gifts parents can give their children is the loving perspectives of their uniqueness and value. A great example is to put together a "blessing packet." You don't need to call it that; you can name it anything you like, such as "Words to Live By," "Chicken Soup for _____'s Soul," or, "A Hundred Things We Love about _____." The point is that you're collecting and delivering messages of encouragement and affirmation for your son or daughter that will strengthen his or her self-worth, identity, and sense of significance and calling.

You'll first need to consider the people who have had the greatest impact on the life of your teen. They can be family members (parents are a must), friends, teachers, mentors, faith leaders, or others who offer a blessing in the form of a letter. As you recruit these VIPs, suggest they share special qualities, memories, inspirational thoughts, pictures, and the like. The purpose is to collect a wide array of well wishes that honor your teen. Then, at an appropriate time, give them an envelope containing these private letters.

Some schools in our area arrange for this at a junior or senior class retreat. It is incredibly powerful. And, it offers you, the parent, an opportunity to say the things you wish you had said or said more. It's especially meaningful for the parents who are less expressive (often fathers). Be forewarned, it can be an incredibly emotional experience for the parent. (Having done two myself, I can personally attest to that!) But, it's a gift we not only give our children, but also to ourselves.

This keepsake is a profound blessing to your children. You don't have to wait until launch time, but it's a great parting gift that honors your teen at this critical time of life.

» *Have a "Rite of Passage" event.* Who doesn't love a great party? During the teen years, we have many opportunities to celebrate the passing of the torch from one life stage to the next. Different cultures have different ceremonial markers to honor these milestones (e.g., bar mitzvahs, bat mitzvahs, quinceañeras, and baccalaureates) signaling the entering of a new season of life. In this context, you can create such an event marking the transition from adolescence to adulthood (at their 18th birthday, graduation, or a separate celebration). They come in many forms (a celebration or weekend away), but generally include other adults who share their perspectives and well-wishes for the journey ahead. "Men's Weekends" or "Women's Weekends" are great examples, where the men or women in their life share wisdom, encouragement, and inspiration to the new adult. Use your creativity and take advantage of the other adults who figure prominently in the life of your son or daughter.

» *Read* What I Wish I Knew at 18 *together.* Some of the most powerful testimonials we hear are from parents who went through this book with their teen during this final summer or, even in their freshman year of college (via Skype). Having a weekly meal or coffee together to share a chapter at a favorite restaurant or coffee shop has offered many special memories to both "launcher" and "launchee."

Letting your young adult select the topics to discuss and sharing your respective stories will not only impart needed wisdom, but also strengthen your relationship. The success pointers and reflective questions provide that needed "third party catalyst" to trigger heart-to-heart conversations. You may learn to understand your young adult in ways you never imagined.

AND, THEY'RE OFF!

For a host of cultural, familial, and economic reasons, today's young adult faces an even greater transition than in generations past. The statistics are too numerable to list, but a telling one is the pathetic college graduation rates in the U.S. compared with other countries. The fact that so many entering college don't finish reveals their lack of preparation for adulthood and all the responsibility that comes with it.

In many cases, it's because they get off to a rocky start. The first three months after leaving home are vitally important, often setting the tone for the rest of a person's college or career experience. We've all heard the tragic stories of college careers that ended prematurely. Here are some ways you can help set your child up for success:

» *Prepare them for the social adjustment.* The loss of their convenient support structure can be hard to take, especially for those who are reserved by nature. Often, this leads to intense loneliness and getting into the wrong crowd for the sake of making new "friends" quickly. Social impatience and insecurity are huge issues for many transitioning young adults.

Talk about this in advance, so they won't be surprised by loneliness and feelings of isolation. Help them plan some strategies, like introducing themselves and making it a point to meet everyone in their dormitory hall, looking for activity and affinity clubs, working out at the recreation center, studying in the library or student union building, where they can meet people, initiating conversations with other students in their classes, and finding people in their major with whom they can study. All of these strategies help make a big place feel smaller.

» *Help them develop strong disciplines.* Time management, distractions, new responsibilities (laundry!), study planning, variable class schedules, and the like are all new facts of life. Plus, in today's technology-laden world, our devices are providing ever-new forms of distraction that many can't handle. The temptation to be playing video games (or surfing Pinterest) instead of doing homework can be huge—not to mention the new social opportunities.

Help them develop a list of priorities and to become master schedulers. What's important to them? Grades? Fitness? New friends? Spiritual life? Encourage them to look at their priority list daily. Are grades most important? Then homework gets done first. Is fitness most important? Then they should get their workout in before class. It helps having a sense of independence along with the value of discipline.

» *Prepare them for the academic pressure.* Competition is stiffer, grades are fewer (putting more pressure on each exam), professors are less inclined to offer extra credit, and parents are *paying* for this education! Making matters worse is that many parents place unreasonable academic pressure on their young adult to sustain or improve upon his or her high school performance. That's a lot to handle! Many times it takes students a full year to adjust. Like me!

Encourage them to buy and use an academic planner (or app on their phone) that puts all of their exam and assignment due dates, and any extra credit assignments, in ONE PLACE. This way your student can keep track of deadlines and not feel rushed by realizing at the last minute that something is due.

Finally, *What I Wish I Knew at 18* devotes an entire chapter to college academics that might prove helpful to your teen.

» S*et them up for financial success.* It amazes me how many credit card offers our household receives in the mail for our college-age kids—who have no jobs! No wonder we hear of so many young adults who run into problems with credit cards and overspending.

It is a MUST for parents and students to be on the same page with respect to money. If you are funding their college education, be sure they understand their financial responsibilities and how to live within the parameters you establish. Whether they are in college or out in the workforce or military, you can help them set up a list of expenses and create at least a rudimentary budget. Encourage them to set aside spending money for the things they want to buy, so they're not tempted to rely on credit cards.

» *Empower them to persevere through stress and adversity.* With the new responsibilities, opportunities, and environment, many students experience meaningful adversity and challenges for the first time shortly after the launch. The college or first-time career brings with it new pressures and outcomes that can be very disappointing. Many are ill-prepared to deal with it. Yesterday's easy going kid can easily become tomorrow's worrywart.

They need to know they're not alone, they can always reach out by phone, and you will always welcome them when they need a hug or word of encouragement. This is NOT the time to talk about their grades, their student loans, or are-they-looking-for-a-job. This IS the time to speak words of affirmation, encouragement, faith, and hope.

» *Establish a communication strategy.* Be sure to develop mutually agreed upon expectations for communicating after they leave. Regularly scheduled weekly calls during the first year are reasonable. They can always call in the interim, but resist the temptation to initiate frequent calls or texts to check in. As hard as it may be (with our painful curiosity!), that would run counter to your role as an empowering coach.

Bottom Line: Advance preparation for these key adjustments will make all the difference in the world.

***

SO, IT ALL COMES DOWN TO THIS

And, now comes the acid test of your parenting—releasing your control and sending your son or daughter off to soar in adulthood and to live his or her dream.

Are you ready?

Are you confident?

Do they know you're confident?

And, are *they* confident?

Our ability to successfully launch our teens to thrive in adulthood is the result of all of the hard work and preparation that has come before. Their self-confidence as independent adults will frame how well they transition to this next phase of life.

As we empower and confidently release our teens, it helps to remember our own lives at that stage. The fact is, we made SO many mistakes (didn't we?), but eventually we found our way. We learned how to do laundry, schedule our courses, change majors and careers, make new friends, manage our time and money, live on our own, and overcome adversity. Our parents didn't know about all of the micro decisions and mistakes we made (Thank God!), but they managed. And, you will too.

The fact is, we can't control our children's outcomes, but we can prepare them to make wise decisions for their long-term futures. We need to let them find their way, while always being there for sharing, caring, and advice as they seek it.

Then you let go, knowing you've given it your best.

It's as simple and as difficult as that!

THE VIEW FROM THE BACK SEAT

And now your soaring eagle is dancing in the wind—navigating toward his/her destiny in life. Sometimes it's a tailwind, while other times it's a frontal or side wind. They will feel turbulence just like you did, but in different ways and in a different time.

There will come a time when your conversations begin to change—in a great way. Just like the joy you experienced teaching them sports or how to ride a bike—you will now enjoy a new and mature relationship, as they make adult decisions and willingly come to you for advice. You will talk about things you've never discussed before, and they will see your value in new ways. Whether it's how to cook a meal, how to know if the man or woman they've just met could be "the one," how to land that dream job, or how to deal with some adversity, they will seek your wisdom and perspective.

And, you will smile each time, knowing that the relationship you've built along the way is an enduring one. They still need you, but in a different way now. Just as it should be.

But, mostly, you just marvel at the adult you once brought into this world.

You are filled with awe and anticipation—for this eagle is soaring toward its destiny, and you helped launch it.

There isn't a feeling like it in the world.

TAKE FIVE

1. How well-prepared is your teen for the four big changes he/she is about to experience? What are his/her hopes and dreams for the next six months? Is he (or she) optimistic and realistic? Are you?

2. Before the launch, how will you offer well wishes, inspiration, and wisdom from the key people in his or her life?

3. How well-prepared are you to let go with confidence and set him or her up for a strong, positive departure?

4. What points from this chapter do you especially feel you need to communicate in terms of advice, expectations, and wisdom to ensure a strong start?

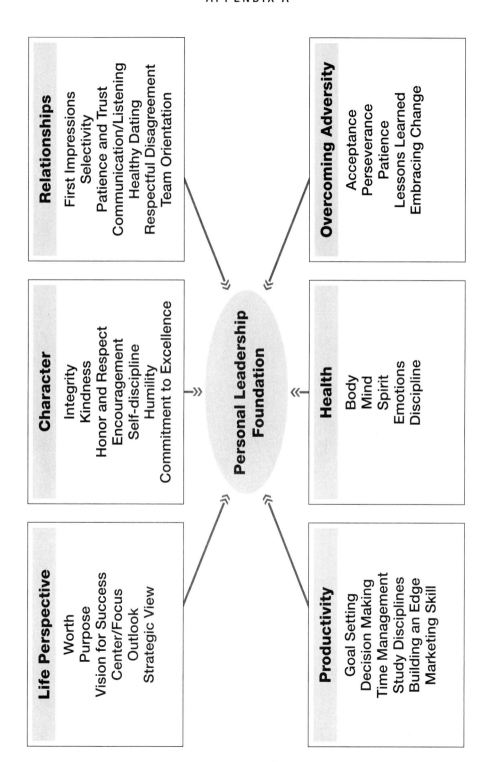

APPENDIX B

109 SUCCESS POINTERS FROM
What I Wish I Knew at 18: Life Lessons for the Road Ahead

LIFE PERSPECTIVE

Discover your purpose and inspiration ⌃ Build a living legacy ⌃ Direct your life toward others ⌃ Live life without regrets ⌃ Don't define success by riches ⌃ Diversify your life ⌃ Don't allow work to consume your life ⌃ Plan, practice, and persevere to succeed ⌃ Take risks—even if you might fail ⌃ See the glass as half full ⌃ Control what you can, but accept what you can't ⌃ Value the ride, not just the outcome ⌃ Embrace change as an opportunity ⌃ Commit to being a life-long learner ⌃ Allow time to reflect ⌃ Immerse yourself in the beauty of God's creation

CHARACTER

Demonstrate your capacity to love ⌃ Cultivate a servant's heart ⌃ Be pro-actively nice ⌃ Preserve your reputation and integrity at all costs ⌃ When facing risky situations, ask how your conscience will feel tomorrow ⌃ Stand up for your beliefs and values with conviction ⌃ Give everything your best ⌃ Don't make promises you can't keep ⌃ Take responsibility for your mistakes and shortfalls ⌃ Choose humility over self-pride ⌃ Solicit and embrace constructive feedback ⌃ Laugh often ⌃ Don't whine . . . just do it! ⌃ Be an encourager rather than a critic and always look for the best in people ⌃ Don't say something about someone else that you wouldn't mind them overhearing ⌃ Be on "role model behavior" around kids

RELATIONSHIPS AND COMMUNICATION

Put relationships before things ⌃ Express yourself! ⌃ Get connected with others who share your interests and values ⌃ Steer clear of destructive people ⌃ First impressions are huge ⌃ Know your audience ⌃ Be inquisitive when meeting others ⌃ Enthusiasm is contagious ⌃ Smile . . . your countenance matters! ⌃ Notice how others react to you ⌃ How you say it can matter more than what you say ⌃ Talk it out, don't write it out ⌃ Be an inspiring team player ⌃ Regularly show appreciation and gratitude toward others ⌃ Strive to be an "agreeable disagreer" ⌃ Choose reconciliation over grudges whenever possible

SPIRITUAL LIFE

Invest in your spiritual growth ⌃ Seek God's wisdom in matters big and small ⌃ Count your blessings ⌃ Reserve time for daily reflection ⌃ Be a wise steward and cheerful giver ⌃ Connect with a worship family ⌃ Develop an accountability relationship with a trusted friend ⌃ Keep the faith during times of trial

HANDLING ADVERSITY

Accept that adversity is a part of life ⌃ Adversity can be preparation for greater things and often makes sense in retrospect ⌃ Day follows night ⌃ Release your pain through prayer, loved ones, and exercise ⌃ Take seemingly insurmountable challenges one step at a time ⌃ Take charge of your worries ⌃ Don't make an important decision while you're upset—sleep on it ⌃ Seek opportunities to help others in even worse shape

MISCELLANEOUS

Set and periodically assess your goals ⌃ Plan, don't procrastinate ⌃ Time is precious . . . use it wisely ⌃ Become a masterful decision maker ⌃ Celebrate your victories and learn from your defeats ⌃ Don't let technology control your life ⌃ Learn to speak comfortably in groups ⌃ Be a discerning skeptic of all you read and hear ⌃ Drive defensively

COLLEGE ACADEMICS

Excelling is about planning, preparing, and performing

CAREER SELECTION AND ADVANCEMENT

Choose your major/career after conducting a comprehensive assessment of yourself and potential career matches ⌃ Consider if it's a career, hobby, or volunteer opportunity ⌃ Build a winning competitive edge ⌃ Seek the wisdom of experienced pros ⌃ Demonstrate the qualities that employers value ⌃ Learn to persuasively market yourself ⌃ Likeability during the interview is huge ⌃ Consider career advancement opportunities when evaluating offers ⌃ The secret to a glowing performance evaluation! ⌃ Diversify your contributions to build your value and win promotions

LOVE AND MARRIAGE

Recognize the difference between love and lust ⌃ Love takes time . . . and timing! ⌃ Take a "3D approach" to dating ⌃ Choose your spouse as a forever decision ⌃ Fully explore your compatibility before committing ⌃ Don't expect your spouse to change his/her ways ⌃ Maintain your friendships after marriage ⌃ Marriage is a partnership that requires continual investment ⌃ Keywords for a successful marriage ⌃ Have children when you're married and ready ⌃ Commit to making these life choices to avoid poverty

MANAGING YOUR FINANCES

Commit to your financial literacy ⌃ Strive to become a wise steward, disciplined saver, prudent consumer, cautious debtor, and cheerful giver ⌃ Beware . . . even those with substantial assets can go bankrupt! ⌃ Live within your means and generate positive cash flow ⌃ Create regular cash flow statements and analyze your spending ⌃ Use credit sparingly and wisely ⌃ Develop a financial plan that reflects your short-and long-term goals ⌃ Understand your ability to handle risk and invest accordingly ⌃ Invest early, regularly, and as much as you can in a diversified, long-term strategy ⌃ Build an emergency fund for unforeseen circumstances ⌃ Grow your wealth patiently ⌃ Build and maintain a good credit rating ⌃ Be the only you

APPENDIX C
FINANCIAL SUCCESS POINTERS FOR LIFE

MANAGING IT:

» Become financially literate regarding the economy, investing, budgeting, debt, and banking
» Be a disciplined planner, skillful earner, wise investor, prudent consumer, cautious debtor, and cheerful giver, and always "live within your means"
» Grow your wealth *patiently*

EARNING IT:

» Select your career *after* comprehensively evaluating your interests, skills, preferences, training requirements, and the employment outlook
» Validate your choice by speaking with actual practitioners
» Build your competitive edge
» Learn to persuasively market yourself
» Build your value in the eyes of your employer

DISTRIBUTING IT:

» Give, invest, then spend (not the reverse!); conservative rule is 10/20/70%
» Develop a *budget* and regularly analyze your spending
» Spend less than you earn to generate "*positive cash flow*"
» Resist the temptation to "keep up with the Joneses"
» Understand the difference between *fixed*, *variable*, and *periodic* expenses
» Avoid high fixed expenses (keep housing costs < 35%) that can't be reduced
» Save up for major expenditures and use debt sparingly
» Avoid credit card purchases that can't be paid off at month-end
» Resist the temptation to impulse buy; be a value conscious consumer

INVESTING IT:

» Invest *early, regularly,* and *as much* as you can in a *globally diversified, long-term investment program* according to your *risk profile* ($12.15 a day from age 23 at 6% annually makes you a millionaire at 65!)

» Assess your *risk-tolerance* and develop an appropriate *asset-allocation* (% in stocks/bonds); it changes as you age with a ballpark of 100 minus your age in stocks

» Think buy low, sell high, and avoid taking more risk when the market is high/bailing out when markets are down; resist the temptation to "time the market"

» Avoid chasing hot investments and buying on tips/rumors

» Build an *emergency fund* equal to 4-6 months of expenses; then develop a monthly investment program for your life

BANKING IT:

» Develop a strong *credit rating* and be someone your banker will lend money to with total confidence! That means having a strong *balance sheet* and positive and rising *net worth* (assets minus debts).

» Understand the difference between debit and credit cards and avoid building large credit card balances like the plague!

» Regularly balance your checking account.

» Avoid identity theft through safekeeping your private information (PINs, Social Security Number, financial statements) and avoid late-night ATM visits

APPENDIX D
PARENTING CHECKLIST:
PREPARING TEENS TO THRIVE IN ADULTHOOD

LIFE PERSPECTIVE:

☐ Do they understand their unique gifts, talents, passions, and worth?

☐ Do they know how to live life *strategically* and with discipline and purpose?

☐ Are they committed to making a positive difference in the world NOW?

☐ Are they guided by an *honorable* definition of "success?"

☐ Are they committed to developing a wide range of interests?

☐ Are they willing to take risks, even if they might not succeed?

☐ Do they project a positive, can-do attitude?

☐ Do they accept that life isn't necessarily fair and avoid complaining?

☐ Do they understand that successful people plan, practice, and persevere?

☐ Are they adaptable to changing circumstances?

CHARACTER:

☐ Do they readily demonstrate love, compassion, and service to others?

☐ Are they guided by integrity in their actions and words?

☐ Do they stand up for their beliefs and values with conviction?

☐ Are they committed to giving everything their best effort?

☐ Do they take full responsibility for their mistakes and shortfalls?

☐ Do they demonstrate humility in their successes and recognize others?

☐ Are they open to receiving constructive feedback?

☐ Do they serve as an encourager, rather than a critic, to others?

☐ Do they act as a role model when around younger people?

RELATIONSHIPS AND COMMUNICATION:

☐ Do they prioritize relationships with others over possessions and power?

☐ Are they comfortable expressing their feelings and emotions to others?

☐ Do they build friendships with people who share their values, beliefs, and interests?

☐ Do they avoid destructive, negative people who don't have their interests at heart and understand that everyone is not meant to be their friend?

☐ Do they know how to make a great first impression?

☐ Do they understand how to gradually cultivate friendships based on mutual trust?

☐ Do they demonstrate excellent listening skills and fully engage in conversation?

☐ Do they regularly show appreciation and gratitude toward others?

☐ Do they know how to disagree in an agreeable manner?

HANDLING ADVERSITY/SPIRITUAL LIFE:

☐ Are they prepared to accept that adversity happens, builds our character, and often makes sense after the fact?

☐ Do they know how to release stress and pain in a healthy and patient manner?

☐ Are they committed to learning from their mistakes?

☐ Are they committed to keeping their faith even during times of trial?

☐ Do they count their blessings and demonstrate a grateful heart even in trials?

☐ Do they reserve time for daily reflection?

☐ Will they prioritize connecting with a worship community after high school?

☐ Do they have an accountability relationship with a trusted friend?

PERSONAL PRODUCTIVITY:

☐ Are they an effective goal-setter, planner, time-manager, and decision-maker?

☐ Are they a responsible and self-disciplined user of technology?

☐ Are they comfortable speaking in groups and leading discussions?

☐ Are they discerning and skeptical of what they read and hear in the news media?

☐ Do they have a disciplined study method that works in high-pressure situations?

CAREER SELECTION AND ADVANCEMENT:

☐ Do they know how to comprehensively assess their interests, skills, lifestyle preferences, and training desires to select a well-matched career?

☐ Do they understand how to build a winning competitive edge and effectively market themselves to potential employers?

☐ Do they fully understand the qualities that employers value in their star employees?

☐ Do they know the secret to a glowing performance evaluation and how to become an indispensable employee?

LOVE AND MARRIAGE:

☐ Do they understand that love takes time and the right timing?

☐ Do they know that the keys to responsible dating involve being *discriminating*, *discerning*, and *deliberate*?

☐ Will they approach marriage as a truly *forever* decision?

☐ Are they committed to fully examining their compatibility before marrying?

☐ Do they understand that marriage is a partnership in which their spouse comes *first*?

☐ Do they know the key qualities of successful, long-term marriages?

☐ Are they committed to having children ONLY when they're married AND financially and emotionally ready?

☐ Do they understand that the three best ways to avoid poverty are to graduate from high school, not marry before 20, and only have children *after* they marry?

FINANCIAL MANAGEMENT:

☐ Do they understand the basics of being financially literate and how to be a wise steward, productive earner, prudent consumer, cautious debtor, and disciplined saver and cheerful giver?

☐ Do they know how to live within their means and manage a budget?

☐ Do they know how to prudently use credit and to pay off their balances monthly?

☐ Do they know the importance of investing early, regularly, and as much as possible in a disciplined and diversified long-term investment program?

☐ Do they understand the workings of the economy and financial markets?

☐ Do they know how to invest and manage their bank accounts?

☐ Do they know the importance of giving first, investing second, and spending last?

☐ Do they know how to build a solid credit rating?

☐ Do they know the ways to avoid identity theft?

PARENTING STYLE AND UPCOMING TRANSITION:

☐ Are you adapting your parenting style from "control" to "influence?"

☐ Do they know how much you love them, value them, and *believe* in them?

☐ Are you actively finding ways to seek out their opinions and help with decisions?

☐ Do you regularly share time together at the time and place of *their* choosing?

☐ Are you prepared to let them go and be their "encouragers in chief?"

☐ Have you shared the key transition risks with them: social impatience, lack of study disciplines, damaging recreational habits, lack of a support network and spiritual life, excessive personal performance stress, and financial irresponsibility?

APPENDIX E
PERSONAL BALANCE SHEET: ABBREVIATED SAMPLE

ASSETS:	CONSTRAINTS:
PHYSICAL	
Speed, strength, agility, football	Asthma
MENTAL/INTELLIGENCE	
Analytical, decision-making, math, comprehension, science, 3.7 GPA	Prone to excessive detail
BEHAVIORAL/PSYCHOLOGICAL/PERSONALITY/EMOTIONAL	
Leader, decisive, goal-oriented, mature, approachable, confident, even-tempered, outgoing, persuasive	Perfectionist, demanding
SUPPORT SYSTEM	
Married and loving parents, five role model adults/ mentors, core group of four close friends	Family finances, mom's health
EXPERIENTIAL	
Three part-time jobs, public speaking, Mission trips, youth mentor, Rotary Leadership award winner, FBLA, Football team captain, ASB	Haven't traveled much, no commercial job experience — jobs have been for friends/family
NETWORK	
Current/past employers, FBLA advisor, Rotary president, football coaches, ASB advisor	All ambassadors are local
SPIRITUAL/INSPIRATIONAL/VALUES	
Strong faith, kind, integrity, generous, loyal, service-minded, encouraging, overcame asthma adversity	Too hard on self when makes mistakes
INTERESTS	
Football, skiing, hiking, watersports, Youth mentoring/coaching, electronics	
PASSIONS AND DREAMS	
Start an electronics business, Master's, married with a few kids, ability to serve on mission-related overseas trips to help people/businesses in developing nations, volunteer football coach, climb Mt. Rainier	

ENDNOTES

1. Lyndsey Layton, "High School Graduation Rate Rises in U.S.," *The Washington Post*, March 1, 2012. http://articles.washingtonpost.com/2012-03-19/local/35448541_1_grad-nation-graduation-rates-robert-balfanz. Accessed 2013-8-12.

2. The Organisation for Economic Co-operation and Development (OECD)

http://www.oecd.org/edu/CN%20-%20United%20States.pdf. Accessed 2013-8-12.

3. Bureau of Labor Statistics, U.S Department of Labor, Press Release, August 2, 2013. http://www.bls.gov/news.release/pdf/empsit.pdf. Accessed 2013-8-21.

4. performed by Herman's Hermits and written by Sam Cooke, Herb Alpert, and Lou Adler.

5. Amy Chua, "Why Chinese Mothers Are Superior," The Wall Street Journal, January 8, 2001. http://online.wsj.com/article/SB10001424052748704111504576059713528698754.html. Accessed 2013-8-27.

6. Mann M, Hosman CM, Schaalma HP, de Vries NK. Self-esteem in a broad-spectrum approach for mental health promotion. Health Educ Res. 2004;19(4):357–372. [PubMed]

7. Waddell GR. Labor-Market Consequences of Poor Attitude and Low Self-Esteem in Youth. Economic Inquiry. 2006;44(1):69–97.

8. Brown, B. B. (2004). Adolescents' relationships with peers. In R. M. Lerner & L. Steinberg (Eds.), *Handbook of Adolescent Psychology, 2nd edition* (pp. 363-394). New York: Wiley.

9. Northwest Family Services. *Talk to Them.* "Media Influences on Youth." http://www.talktothem.org/en/want-to-know/teens-and-the-media.html. Accessed 2013-7-13.

10. nbcnews.com (2013-8-7-2006). "Dirty Song Lyrics Can Prompt Early Teen Sex." http://www.nbcnews.com/id/14227775/ns/health-sexual_health/t/dirty-song-lyrics-can-prompt-early-teen-sex/#.UdQaauvqJ6l. Accessed 2013-7-3.

11. Ibid

12. Caralee J. Adams, "Soft Skills Pushed As Part of College Readiness," *Education Week*, November 13, 2012, http://www.edweek.org/ew/articles/2012/11/14/12softskills_ep.h32.html?tkn=XVRFh7IBpDX85KcZnMxiyWHCN4zCVHWSXc3A&cmp=ENL-EU-NEWS2. Accessed 2013-8-21.

13. Dennis Trittin, *What I Wish I Knew at 18: Life Lessons for the Road Ahead*, LifeSmart Publishing, Gig Harbor, WA: 2010. www.dennistrittin.com, 132, 133.

WE'D LOVE TO HEAR FROM YOU!

We hope you enjoyed our book! Please keep in touch.
You can find us:

On our websites:
www.parentingforthelaunch.com,
www.dennistrittin.com

By email:
dtrittin@dennistrittin.com,
arlyn@lifesmartpublishing.com

By signing up for our email newsletter:
http://www.dennistrittin.com/newsletter.aspx

On Facebook:
www.facebook.com/parentingforthelaunch
www.facebook.com/dennistrittinfan
("Like" us!)

On Twitter:
www.twitter.com/parent4launch
www.twitter.com/arlynlawrence
("Follow" us!)

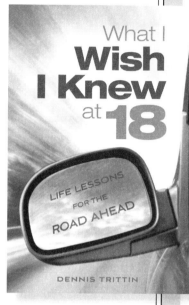